Online Entrepreneurship Success Roadmap

While every precaution has been taken in the preparation of this book, the publisher assumes no responsibility for errors or omissions, or for damages resulting from the use of the information contained herein.

ONLINE ENTREPRENEURSHIP: SUCCESS ROADMAP

First edition. November 15, 2023.

Copyright © 2023 imed el arbi.

ISBN: 979-8223700852

Written by imed el arbi.

The Online Entrepreneur's Mindset

1.1 Understanding the Online Business Landscape

I n today's digital age, the online business landscape offers endless opportunities for entrepreneurs to create successful ventures. The internet has revolutionized the way we do business, providing a global platform for individuals to connect, engage, and transact. Understanding the intricacies of this landscape is crucial for aspiring online entrepreneurs who wish to navigate the digital realm effectively.

1.1.1 The Evolution of Online Business

THE ONLINE BUSINESS landscape has evolved significantly over the years. From the early days of the internet, where websites were static and limited in functionality, to the dynamic and interactive platforms we see today, the digital world has undergone a remarkable transformation. E-commerce, social media, and digital marketing have become integral components of the online business ecosystem, enabling entrepreneurs to reach a global audience and drive growth like never before.

1.1.2 The Power of Online Entrepreneurship

ONLINE ENTREPRENEURSHIP offers unique advantages that traditional brick-and-mortar businesses may not possess. The ability to operate remotely, reach a global customer base, and leverage digital tools and technologies are just a few of the benefits that online entrepreneurs enjoy. The internet has leveled the playing field, allowing individuals with innovative ideas and a strong work ethic to compete with established businesses and disrupt industries.

1.1.3 Identifying Online Business Opportunities

TO SUCCEED IN THE ONLINE business landscape, it is essential to identify and capitalize on opportunities. This requires a deep understanding of market trends, consumer behavior, and emerging technologies. Conducting thorough market research and staying updated with industry news and developments can help entrepreneurs identify gaps in the market and create innovative solutions to meet customer needs.

1.1.4 Navigating the Competitive Landscape

WHILE THE ONLINE BUSINESS landscape offers immense opportunities, it is also highly competitive. Entrepreneurs must be prepared to navigate through a crowded marketplace and differentiate themselves from competitors. Developing a unique value proposition, understanding target audience preferences, and delivering exceptional customer experiences are key strategies for standing out in a crowded digital marketplace.

1.1.5 Embracing Technological Advancements

TECHNOLOGY PLAYS A pivotal role in the online business landscape. As an online entrepreneur, it is crucial to stay updated with the latest technological advancements and leverage them to your advantage. From website development and search engine optimization to social media advertising and data analytics, technology empowers entrepreneurs to streamline operations, enhance customer experiences, and drive business growth.

1.1.6 Adapting to Changing Consumer Behavior

CONSUMER BEHAVIOR IS constantly evolving in response to technological advancements and societal changes. Online entrepreneurs must stay attuned to these shifts and adapt their strategies accordingly. Understanding consumer preferences, embracing new communication channels, and delivering personalized experiences are essential for building strong customer relationships and driving long-term success.

1.1.7 The Global Reach of Online Business

ONE OF THE MOST SIGNIFICANT advantages of online entrepreneurship is the ability to reach a global audience. The internet has eliminated geographical barriers, allowing entrepreneurs to connect with customers from all corners of the world. However, expanding into international markets requires careful consideration of cultural nuances, local regulations, and market dynamics. Entrepreneurs must develop strategies to effectively target and engage with diverse audiences.

1.1.8 Embracing Innovation and Disruption

INNOVATION AND DISRUPTION are at the core of successful online businesses. Entrepreneurs must embrace a mindset of continuous improvement and be open to exploring new ideas and approaches. By challenging the status quo and pushing boundaries, online entrepreneurs can create unique value propositions and disrupt traditional industries.

1.1.9 The Importance of Collaboration and Networking

COLLABORATION AND NETWORKING are vital for online entrepreneurs to thrive in the digital landscape. Building relationships with industry peers, influencers, and potential partners can open doors to new opportunities, provide valuable insights, and foster growth. Engaging in online communities, attending industry events, and participating in collaborative projects can help entrepreneurs expand their network and gain exposure.

1.1.10 The Future of Online Entrepreneurship

THE ONLINE BUSINESS landscape is constantly evolving, driven by technological advancements and changing consumer behaviors. As an online entrepreneur, it is crucial to stay agile and adaptable to navigate the future successfully. Embracing emerging technologies, staying updated with industry trends, and continuously learning and evolving are key strategies for long-term success in the ever-changing digital world.

Understanding the online business landscape is the first step towards becoming a successful online entrepreneur. By grasping the evolution of online business, identifying opportunities, embracing technological advancements, and adapting to changing consumer behaviors, aspiring entrepreneurs can position themselves for growth and thrive in the digital realm. In the next chapter, we will explore the mindset required for online entrepreneurship and how to develop a growth mindset that will propel you towards success.

1.2 Developing a Growth Mindset

———

In the fast-paced and ever-evolving world of online entrepreneurship, developing a growth mindset is crucial for success. A growth mindset is the belief that abilities and intelligence can be developed through dedication, hard work, and continuous learning. It is the mindset of embracing challenges, persisting in the face of setbacks, and seeing failures as opportunities for growth. By cultivating a growth mindset, online entrepreneurs can overcome obstacles, adapt to changes, and unlock their full potential.

1.2.1 Embracing Challenges as Opportunities

ONE OF THE KEY ASPECTS of developing a growth mindset is embracing challenges as opportunities for growth. Instead of shying away from difficult tasks or avoiding risks, online entrepreneurs with a growth mindset see challenges as a chance to learn, improve, and expand their capabilities. They understand that by stepping out of their comfort zones and taking on new challenges, they can acquire new skills, gain valuable experience, and ultimately achieve greater success.

When faced with a challenge, a growth-minded entrepreneur will approach it with a positive attitude and a willingness to learn. They understand that setbacks and failures are not indicators of their abilities or worth but rather stepping stones on the path to success. They view challenges as opportunities to stretch their limits, develop resilience, and discover innovative solutions. By embracing challenges, online entrepreneurs can continuously improve their skills and stay ahead in the competitive digital landscape.

1.2.2 Cultivating a Passion for Learning

A GROWTH MINDSET IS closely tied to a passion for learning. Online entrepreneurs with a growth mindset understand the importance of continuous education and skill development. They actively seek out opportunities to expand their knowledge, whether through reading books, attending webinars, taking online courses, or networking with industry experts. They understand that staying updated with the latest trends, technologies, and strategies is essential for staying competitive and driving innovation in their online businesses.

Cultivating a passion for learning involves being open-minded and curious. Growth-minded entrepreneurs are not afraid to ask questions, seek feedback, and explore new ideas. They understand that there is always room for improvement and that learning is a lifelong journey. By embracing a mindset of continuous learning, online entrepreneurs can adapt to changes, seize new opportunities, and stay ahead of the curve in the dynamic digital landscape.

1.2.3 Embracing Failure as a Learning Opportunity

FAILURE IS AN INEVITABLE part of the entrepreneurial journey, especially in the online realm. However, online entrepreneurs with a growth mindset view failure as a valuable learning opportunity rather than a setback. They understand that failure is not a reflection of their abilities or potential but rather a chance to learn, grow, and improve.

When faced with failure, growth-minded entrepreneurs analyze the situation, identify the lessons learned, and make adjustments for future endeavors. They do not let failure define them or discourage them from pursuing their goals. Instead, they use failure as a stepping stone towards success. By embracing failure and learning from it, online entrepreneurs can refine their strategies, develop resilience, and ultimately achieve their desired outcomes.

1.2.4 Developing a Positive and Resilient Attitude

A GROWTH MINDSET IS characterized by a positive and resilient attitude. Online entrepreneurs with a growth mindset understand that setbacks and challenges are part of the journey and that success is not achieved overnight. They maintain a positive outlook even in the face of adversity and setbacks. They believe in their abilities and have confidence in their capacity to overcome obstacles and achieve their goals.

Developing resilience is also a crucial aspect of a growth mindset. Resilient entrepreneurs bounce back from failures, setbacks, and rejections. They do not let temporary defeats discourage them or derail their progress. Instead, they learn from their experiences, adapt their strategies, and persevere towards their goals. By developing a positive and resilient attitude, online entrepreneurs can navigate the ups and downs of the online business landscape with confidence and determination.

1.2.5 Seeking Feedback and Collaboration

ONLINE ENTREPRENEURS with a growth mindset understand the value of feedback and collaboration. They actively seek feedback from customers, mentors, and peers to gain insights into their strengths and areas for improvement. They view feedback as an opportunity to grow and refine their strategies. By embracing feedback, they can make informed decisions, enhance their products or services, and better meet the needs of their target audience.

Collaboration is also an essential aspect of a growth mindset. Growth-minded entrepreneurs understand that they cannot achieve success alone. They actively seek opportunities to collaborate with others, whether through partnerships, joint ventures, or networking events. By collaborating with like-minded individuals, they can leverage each other's strengths, share knowledge and resources, and accelerate their growth.

In conclusion, developing a growth mindset is essential for online entrepreneurs to thrive in the dynamic and competitive digital landscape. By embracing challenges, cultivating a passion for learning, embracing failure as a learning opportunity, developing a positive and resilient attitude, and seeking feedback and collaboration, online entrepreneurs can unlock their full potential and achieve long-term success.

1.3 Overcoming Challenges and Failure

―――

S tarting an online business can be an exciting and rewarding endeavor, but it is not without its challenges. In this section, we will explore some of the common obstacles that online entrepreneurs face and strategies for overcoming them. We will also discuss the importance of embracing failure as a learning opportunity and developing resilience to bounce back from setbacks.

1.3.1 Embracing Failure as a Learning Opportunity

FAILURE IS AN INEVITABLE part of any entrepreneurial journey, and it is important to view it as a valuable learning opportunity rather than a setback. Many successful entrepreneurs have experienced multiple failures before achieving their breakthroughs. It is through these failures that they learn valuable lessons, refine their strategies, and ultimately achieve success.

When faced with failure, it is crucial to adopt a growth mindset. Instead of dwelling on the negative aspects of the experience, focus on what can be learned from it. Ask yourself questions like: What went wrong? What could have been done differently? How can this failure be turned into an opportunity for growth?

By reframing failure as a stepping stone to success, you can approach challenges with a positive and proactive mindset. Embrace the lessons learned from failure and use them to improve your strategies and decision-making in the future.

1.3.2 Developing Resilience and Persistence

RESILIENCE AND PERSISTENCE are key traits that successful online entrepreneurs possess. Building a business takes time, effort, and perseverance. There will be times when things don't go as planned, and setbacks can be discouraging. However, it is important to stay resilient and persistent in the face of adversity.

One way to develop resilience is by cultivating a strong support network. Surround yourself with like-minded individuals who understand the challenges of entrepreneurship and can provide guidance and encouragement. Join online communities, attend networking events, and seek out mentors who can offer valuable insights and support.

Another important aspect of resilience is self-care. Running a business can be demanding, both mentally and physically. Take time to recharge and prioritize your well-being. Engage in activities that bring you joy and help you relax. This will not only help you stay resilient but also enhance your creativity and problem-solving abilities.

Persistence is also crucial in overcoming challenges. It is natural to face obstacles along the way, but it is important to persevere and keep moving forward. Break down your goals into smaller, manageable tasks and celebrate each milestone achieved. This will help you stay motivated and focused on the bigger picture.

1.3.3 Strategies for Overcoming Challenges

WHILE CHALLENGES ARE inevitable, there are strategies you can employ to overcome them and keep your online business on track. Here are a few key strategies to consider:

1. Identify the Root Cause

WHEN FACED WITH A CHALLENGE, it is important to identify the root cause rather than just addressing the symptoms. Take the time to analyze the situation and understand what factors contributed to the challenge. This will enable you to develop targeted solutions and prevent similar issues from arising in the future.

2. Seek Support and Expertise

DON'T BE AFRAID TO ask for help when needed. Reach out to mentors, industry experts, or fellow entrepreneurs who have faced similar challenges. Their insights and experiences can provide valuable guidance and help you navigate through difficult situations.

3. Adapt and Innovate

THE ONLINE BUSINESS landscape is constantly evolving, and it is important to adapt and innovate to stay ahead.

Embrace change and be open to new ideas and technologies. Continuously evaluate your strategies and make necessary adjustments to keep up with the ever-changing digital landscape.

4. Learn from Customer Feedback

YOUR CUSTOMERS ARE a valuable source of feedback and insights. Actively seek feedback from your customers and use it to improve your products, services, and overall customer experience. By listening to your customers and addressing their needs, you can build stronger relationships and enhance your business's reputation.

5. Stay Positive and Motivated

MAINTAINING A POSITIVE mindset is crucial when facing challenges. Surround yourself with positivity and motivation. Read books, listen to podcasts, or attend seminars that inspire and uplift you. Remember why you started your online business in the first place and stay focused on your long-term goals.

Conclusion

OVERCOMING CHALLENGES and failure is an integral part of the online entrepreneurial journey. By embracing failure as a learning opportunity, developing resilience and persistence, and employing effective strategies, you can navigate through obstacles and achieve success. Remember that challenges are not roadblocks but stepping stones to growth and innovation. Stay focused, stay motivated, and keep pushing forward on your path to online entrepreneurship success.

1.4 Building Resilience and Persistence

Building a successful online business requires more than just technical skills and knowledge. It also requires a strong mindset and the ability to overcome challenges and setbacks. In this section, we will explore the importance of building resilience and persistence as an online entrepreneur.

1.4.1 The Importance of Resilience

RESILIENCE IS THE ABILITY to bounce back from setbacks, adapt to change, and keep moving forward. In the world of online entrepreneurship, resilience is crucial because you will inevitably face obstacles and setbacks along the way. Whether it's a failed marketing campaign, a negative customer review, or a technical glitch on your website, these challenges can be discouraging. However, it's important to remember that setbacks are a natural part of the entrepreneurial journey.

Resilience allows you to view setbacks as opportunities for growth and learning. Instead of dwelling on failures, resilient entrepreneurs use them as stepping stones to success. They learn from their mistakes, make necessary adjustments, and keep pushing forward. Resilience also helps you maintain a positive mindset, which is essential for staying motivated and focused on your goals.

1.4.2 Cultivating Persistence

PERSISTENCE IS THE ability to stay committed to your goals and keep taking action, even when faced with obstacles and setbacks. It is the driving force that keeps you going when things get tough. Without persistence, it's easy to give up at the first sign of difficulty.

As an online entrepreneur, persistence is crucial because building a successful business takes time and effort. It's not uncommon to face challenges that make you question whether it's worth it. However, persistent entrepreneurs understand that success rarely happens overnight. They are willing to put in the work and stay dedicated to their vision, even when progress is slow.

Cultivating persistence requires a combination of determination, discipline, and self-belief. It's about setting clear goals, breaking them down into manageable tasks, and consistently taking action towards them. It's also about staying focused on your long-term vision and reminding yourself of why you started in the first place.

1.4.3 Strategies for Building Resilience and Persistence

BUILDING RESILIENCE and persistence is a continuous process that requires effort and practice. Here are some strategies to help you develop these essential qualities as an online entrepreneur:

1. Embrace a Growth Mindset

A GROWTH MINDSET IS the belief that your abilities and intelligence can be developed through dedication and hard work. Embracing a growth mindset allows you to see challenges as opportunities for growth and learning. It helps you view setbacks as temporary and believe in your ability to overcome them. By adopting a growth mindset, you can build resilience and persistence in the face of adversity.

2. Set Realistic Expectations

SETTING REALISTIC EXPECTATIONS is crucial for maintaining resilience and persistence. Understand that building a successful online business takes time and effort. It's important to set achievable goals and break them down into smaller milestones. Celebrate each milestone as a step towards your ultimate vision, and don't get discouraged if progress is slower than expected.

3. Learn from Failure

FAILURE IS A NATURAL part of the entrepreneurial journey. Instead of viewing failure as a setback, see it as an opportunity to learn and grow. Analyze what went wrong, identify the lessons learned, and make necessary adjustments. By embracing failure as a learning experience, you can build resilience and persistence in the face of future challenges.

4. Seek Support and Accountability

BUILDING RESILIENCE and persistence can be
challenging on your own. Surround yourself with a supportive
network of fellow entrepreneurs, mentors, or coaches who can
provide guidance and encouragement. They can offer valuable
insights, share their own experiences, and hold you accountable
to your goals. Having a support system can help you stay
motivated and resilient during difficult times.

5. Practice Self-Care

TAKING CARE OF YOUR physical and mental well-being
is essential for building resilience and persistence. Make sure to
prioritize self-care activities such as exercise, proper nutrition,
and sufficient rest. Engage in activities that help you relax and
recharge, such as meditation, hobbies, or spending time with
loved ones. By taking care of yourself, you can maintain the
energy and mental clarity needed to persevere through
challenges.

Conclusion

BUILDING RESILIENCE and persistence is essential for
success as an online entrepreneur. By cultivating these qualities,
you can navigate the inevitable challenges and setbacks that
come with building an online business. Embrace a growth
mindset, set realistic expectations, learn from failure, seek
support, and practice self-care. With these strategies, you can

develop the resilience and persistence needed to overcome obstacles and achieve long-term success in the digital world.

rafting Your Vision

2.1 Defining Your Purpose and Values

———

In the fast-paced and ever-evolving world of online entrepreneurship, it is crucial to have a clear understanding of your purpose and values. Defining your purpose and values will serve as the foundation for your online business and guide your decision-making process. It will help you stay focused, motivated, and aligned with your long-term goals. In this section, we will explore the importance of defining your purpose and values and provide practical steps to help you uncover them.

2.1.1 Why Define Your Purpose and Values?

DEFINING YOUR PURPOSE and values is essential for several reasons. Firstly, it gives you a sense of direction and clarity. When you have a clear purpose, you know why you are doing what you are doing. It becomes easier to set goals, make decisions, and prioritize tasks. Your purpose acts as a compass, guiding you through the challenges and uncertainties of the online business landscape.

Secondly, your purpose and values help you differentiate yourself from competitors. In a crowded online marketplace, having a unique selling proposition is crucial. By aligning your purpose and values with your business, you can create a brand that resonates with your target audience. Customers are more likely to connect with businesses that share their values and beliefs.

Lastly, defining your purpose and values provides a sense of fulfillment and satisfaction. When your business is aligned with your personal values, it becomes more than just a means to make money. It becomes a vehicle for making a positive impact and contributing to something greater than yourself. This sense of purpose can fuel your motivation and drive, even during challenging times.

2.1.2 Uncovering Your Purpose

DISCOVERING YOUR PURPOSE is a deeply personal and introspective process. It requires self-reflection, exploration, and a willingness to dig deep. Here are some steps to help you uncover your purpose:

1. Reflect on your passions and interests: Start by identifying the activities and topics that genuinely excite and energize you. What are you naturally drawn to? What do you enjoy doing in your free time? Your passions can provide valuable clues about your purpose.

2. Identify your strengths and skills: Take inventory of your strengths and skills. What are you naturally good at? What unique talents do you possess? Your purpose is often aligned with your natural abilities, as they are indicators of where you can make the most significant impact.

3. Consider your values and beliefs: Reflect on your core

values and beliefs. What principles do you hold dear? What causes or issues are important to you? Your purpose should align with your values, as they will guide your decision-making and shape your business's culture.

4. Explore your life experiences: Look back on your life experiences, both positive and negative. What lessons have you learned? How have these experiences shaped you? Sometimes, our purpose emerges from the challenges we have overcome or the lessons we have learned along the way.

5. Seek feedback from others: Reach out to trusted friends, family members, or mentors and ask for their perspective. Sometimes, others can see our strengths and passions more clearly than we can. Their insights can provide valuable guidance in uncovering your purpose.

2.1.3 Defining Your Values

ONCE YOU HAVE A CLEARER understanding of your purpose, it is essential to define your values. Your values are the guiding principles that shape your behavior and decision-making. They act as a compass, ensuring that you stay true to yourself and your purpose. Here are some steps to help you define your values:

1. Identify your core values: Reflect on the principles that are most important to you. What do you stand for? What qualities do you admire in others? Write down a list of values that resonate with you.

2. Prioritize your values: Review your list of values and prioritize them based on their importance to you. Consider which values are non-negotiable and which ones you are willing to compromise on.

3. Align your values with your purpose: Evaluate how well your values align with your purpose. Do they support and reinforce your purpose, or do they conflict with it? Make adjustments as necessary to ensure alignment.

4. Communicate your values: Once you have defined your values, it is crucial to communicate them clearly to your team, customers, and stakeholders. Your values should be reflected in your brand messaging, marketing materials, and interactions with others.

2.1.4 Creating a Purpose Statement

TO SOLIDIFY YOUR PURPOSE and values, it can be helpful to create a purpose statement. A purpose statement is a concise and powerful declaration that encapsulates your mission and values. It serves as a guiding light for your business and communicates your intentions to others. Here are some tips for creating a purpose statement:

1. Be clear and concise: Keep your purpose statement simple and easy to understand. Avoid jargon or complex language. Aim for a statement that can be easily remembered and communicated.

2. Focus on impact: Emphasize the impact you want to make through your business. How do you want to improve the lives of your customers or contribute to

society? Your purpose statement should convey the positive change you aspire to create.

3. Incorporate your values: Ensure that your purpose statement reflects your core values. It should convey the principles and beliefs that guide your business.

4. Make it aspirational: Your purpose statement should inspire and motivate both you and your team. It should be aspirational, challenging you to reach for greatness and make a significant impact.

Remember, your purpose and values may evolve over time as you gain more experience and insights. Revisit and refine them periodically to ensure they remain aligned with your vision and goals. By defining your purpose and values, you lay a solid foundation for your online business and set yourself up for long-term success.

2.2 Setting SMART Goals

———

In order to achieve success in any endeavor, it is crucial to set clear and actionable goals. This is especially true for online entrepreneurs who operate in a fast-paced and ever-changing digital landscape. Setting SMART goals is a proven method that can help you stay focused, motivated, and on track towards achieving your vision.

2.2.1 What are SMART Goals?

SMART IS AN ACRONYM that stands for Specific, Measurable, Achievable, Relevant, and Time-bound. When setting goals, it is important to ensure that they meet these criteria to increase the likelihood of success.

Specific

A SPECIFIC GOAL IS one that is clear and well-defined. It answers the questions of what, why, and how. Instead of setting a vague goal like "increase sales," a specific goal would be "increase monthly sales by 20% within the next six months." By being specific, you can clearly define what you want to achieve and create a roadmap to get there.

Measurable

A MEASURABLE GOAL IS one that can be quantified or tracked. It allows you to assess your progress and determine whether you are moving in the right direction. For example, if your goal is to increase website traffic, you can set a measurable goal of "increase website traffic by 30% within the next three months." This allows you to track your website analytics and measure the success of your efforts.

Achievable

AN ACHIEVABLE GOAL is one that is realistic and attainable. While it is important to set ambitious goals, it is equally important to ensure that they are within reach. Setting unrealistic goals can lead to frustration and demotivation. By setting achievable goals, you can maintain a sense of progress and momentum. For example, if you are just starting out in your online business, setting a goal to generate a million dollars in revenue within the first month may not be achievable. Instead, you can set a more realistic goal based on your current resources and capabilities.

Relevant

A RELEVANT GOAL IS one that aligns with your overall vision and objectives. It is important to ensure that your goals are relevant to your business and will contribute to its growth and success. Setting goals that are not aligned with your vision can lead to wasted time and resources. Before setting a goal, ask yourself whether it is relevant to your long-term vision and if it will help you move closer to your desired outcome.

Time-bound

A TIME-BOUND GOAL IS one that has a specific deadline or timeframe. Setting a deadline creates a sense of urgency and helps you stay focused and motivated. Without a deadline, goals can easily be pushed aside or forgotten. By setting a time-bound goal, you can create a sense of accountability and ensure that you are taking consistent action towards achieving it.

2.2.2 The Benefits of Setting SMART Goals

SETTING SMART GOALS offers several benefits for online entrepreneurs. Here are some of the key advantages:

Clarity and Focus

BY SETTING SPECIFIC goals, you gain clarity on what you want to achieve and how to get there. This clarity helps you stay focused and avoid getting overwhelmed by the multitude of tasks and opportunities that come your way. With a clear goal in mind, you can prioritize your actions and make decisions that align with your objectives.

Motivation and Accountability

SETTING MEASURABLE and time-bound goals provides a sense of motivation and accountability. When you have a clear target to work towards and a deadline to meet, you are more likely to stay motivated and take consistent action. Additionally, the ability to track your progress and measure your success keeps you accountable and allows you to make adjustments if necessary.

Efficiency and Productivity

SMART GOALS HELP YOU become more efficient and productive in your work. By setting specific and achievable goals, you can focus your time and energy on tasks that directly contribute to your desired outcomes. This eliminates wasted effort and allows you to make the most of your resources.

Adaptability and Flexibility

WHILE SETTING SMART goals provides structure and direction, it is important to remain adaptable and flexible. The digital landscape is constantly evolving, and it is essential to be open to new opportunities and adjust your goals accordingly. By regularly reviewing and reassessing your goals, you can ensure that they remain relevant and aligned with the changing dynamics of your business.

2.2.3 Implementing SMART Goals in Your Online Business

NOW THAT YOU UNDERSTAND the importance and benefits of setting SMART goals, it's time to implement them in your online business. Here are some steps to help you get started:

Step 1: Define Your Vision and Objectives

BEFORE SETTING SMART goals, it is important to have a clear vision and objectives for your online business. Your goals should align with your overall vision and contribute to its realization. Take the time to define your long-term vision and break it down into specific objectives that can be achieved within a certain timeframe.

Step 2: Identify Key Areas for Improvement

IDENTIFY THE KEY AREAS in your business that require improvement or growth. This could include increasing sales, improving website traffic, expanding your customer base, or enhancing your online presence. By focusing on these key areas, you can set goals that directly address your business needs.

Step 3: Set Specific and Measurable Goals

BASED ON THE KEY AREAS you have identified, set specific and measurable goals. Ensure that each goal is clear, well-defined, and can be quantified or tracked. For example, instead of setting a goal to "increase social media engagement," set a goal to "increase social media engagement by 50% within the next three months."

Step 4: Assess Achievability and Relevance

ASSESS THE ACHIEVABILITY and relevance of each goal. Consider your available resources, capabilities, and the current state of your business. Ensure that each goal is realistic and aligned with your overall vision and objectives. If necessary, adjust your goals to make them more attainable and relevant.

Step 5: Set Time-Bound Deadlines

ASSIGN A SPECIFIC DEADLINE or timeframe to each goal. This creates a sense of urgency and helps you stay focused and motivated. Be realistic when setting deadlines and consider the time and effort required to achieve each goal. Regularly review and reassess your deadlines to ensure they remain achievable.

Step 6: Track Progress and Make Adjustments

REGULARLY TRACK YOUR progress towards each goal and measure your success. Use relevant metrics and analytics to assess your performance and make adjustments if necessary. If you find that you are not making sufficient progress towards a goal, identify the reasons why and make the necessary changes to your strategy or approach.

By implementing SMART goals in your online business, you can increase your chances of success and achieve your desired outcomes. Remember to regularly review and update your goals as your business evolves and the digital landscape changes. Stay focused, stay motivated, and stay committed to your vision.

2.3 Creating a Compelling Mission Statement

A mission statement is a concise and powerful statement that defines the purpose and direction of your online business. It serves as a guiding light, outlining your goals, values, and the impact you aim to make in the world. A compelling mission statement not only inspires you but also resonates with your target audience, attracting customers who align with your vision. In this section, we will explore the key elements of creating a compelling mission statement that sets the foundation for your online entrepreneurship journey.

2.3.1 Understanding the Importance of a Mission Statement

A MISSION STATEMENT is more than just a few words on your website or marketing materials. It is a reflection of your business's core values, beliefs, and aspirations. A well-crafted mission statement communicates your purpose to your customers, employees, and stakeholders, helping them understand why your business exists and what it stands for. It provides clarity and direction, guiding your decision-making process and shaping your business strategy.

A compelling mission statement has several benefits for your online business. Firstly, it helps differentiate your brand from competitors by highlighting your unique value proposition.

It also serves as a rallying point for your team, aligning their efforts towards a common goal. Additionally, a mission statement can attract customers who resonate with your values, fostering loyalty and long-term relationships. Finally, it provides a framework for evaluating opportunities and making strategic decisions that align with your business's purpose.

2.3.2 Defining Your Business's Purpose and Values

BEFORE CRAFTING YOUR mission statement, it is crucial to have a clear understanding of your business's purpose and values. Ask yourself why you started your online venture and what you hope to achieve. Consider the impact you want to make in the lives of your customers and the broader community. Reflect on your core values and the principles that guide your decision-making process.

To define your purpose and values, start by brainstorming and jotting down your thoughts. Consider the problems you aim to solve, the needs you want to fulfill, and the values you want to uphold. Think about the unique qualities that set your business apart and the positive change you want to bring to the world. Once you have a list of ideas, distill them into a concise and impactful statement that captures the essence of your business.

2.3.3 Crafting a Clear and Concise Statement

A COMPELLING MISSION statement should be clear, concise, and memorable. It should communicate your business's purpose in a way that resonates with your target audience. Here are some key elements to consider when crafting your mission statement:

1. **Clarity**: Your mission statement should clearly articulate what your business does and the impact it aims to make. Avoid using jargon or complex language that may confuse your audience. Keep it simple and easy to understand.

2. **Conciseness**: A mission statement should be brief and to the point. Aim for a statement that is no longer than a few sentences. This ensures that it is easily digestible and memorable.

3. **Relevance**: Your mission statement should be relevant to your target audience. Consider their needs, desires, and aspirations. Think about how your business can address those needs and make a positive impact in their lives.

4. **Differentiation**: Highlight what sets your business apart from competitors. Emphasize your unique value proposition and the qualities that make your business special. This will help attract customers who resonate with your mission.

5. **Inspiration**: A compelling mission statement should inspire both your team and your customers. It should evoke emotion and create a sense of purpose. Use powerful and positive language that ignites passion and motivates action.

6. **Authenticity**: Your mission statement should reflect the true essence of your business. Be genuine and true to your values. Avoid making generic or vague

statements that could undermine your credibility.

2.3.4 Examples of Compelling Mission Statements

TO HELP YOU UNDERSTAND how to craft a compelling mission statement, here are a few examples from successful online businesses:

1. **Patagonia**: "Build the best product, cause no unnecessary harm, use business to inspire and implement solutions to the environmental crisis."
2. **Warby Parker**: "To offer designer eyewear at a revolutionary price while leading the way for socially conscious businesses."
3. **Tesla**: "To accelerate the world's transition to sustainable energy."
4. **Airbnb**: "To help create a world where you can belong anywhere and where people can live in a place, instead of just traveling to it."

These mission statements are clear, concise, and impactful. They communicate the purpose and values of each business, inspiring both their teams and customers.

2.3.5 Refining and Evolving Your Mission Statement

CREATING A COMPELLING mission statement is not a one-time task. As your business evolves and grows, you may need to refine and update your mission statement to reflect your changing goals and values. Regularly revisit your mission statement to ensure it remains relevant and aligned with your business's direction.

Seek feedback from your team, customers, and stakeholders to gain different perspectives and insights. Consider conducting surveys or interviews to understand how your mission statement resonates with your target audience. Use this feedback to refine and improve your mission statement over time.

Remember, a compelling mission statement is a living document that evolves with your business. Embrace the iterative process of refining and updating it as your online venture progresses.

Conclusion

———

C rafting a compelling mission statement is a crucial step in building a successful online business. It serves as a guiding light, aligning your efforts and attracting customers who resonate with your purpose and values. By defining your business's purpose and values, and crafting a clear and concise statement, you can create a mission statement that inspires both your team and your customers. Regularly revisit and refine your mission statement to ensure it remains relevant and aligned with your business's growth and evolution. With a compelling mission statement, you can set the foundation for long-term success in the online entrepreneurship journey.

2.4 Visualizing Your Success

———

Visualizing your success is a powerful tool that can help you achieve your goals and aspirations as an online entrepreneur. By creating a clear mental image of what you want to achieve, you can align your actions and decisions with your desired outcomes. Visualization allows you to tap into the power of your subconscious mind and harness the law of attraction to manifest your dreams into reality.

2.4.1 The Power of Visualization

VISUALIZATION IS THE process of creating vivid mental images of your desired outcomes. It involves using your imagination to see, hear, and feel the experience of achieving your goals. When you visualize your success, you activate the creative power of your mind and send a clear message to the universe about what you want to attract into your life.

Research has shown that visualization can have a profound impact on performance and goal attainment. Athletes, for example, often use visualization techniques to enhance their performance and improve their chances of success. By mentally rehearsing their actions and outcomes, they create a blueprint for success in their minds.

As an online entrepreneur, visualization can help you in several ways:

1. **Clarifying Your Goals**: Visualization allows you to gain clarity about what you truly want to achieve. By creating a detailed mental image of your desired outcomes, you can define your goals with greater precision and specificity.

2. **Boosting Motivation**: When you visualize your success, you tap into the emotions and feelings associated with achieving your goals. This emotional connection can fuel your motivation and drive, helping you stay focused and committed to your entrepreneurial journey.

3. **Building Confidence**: Visualization can help you build confidence by mentally rehearsing successful outcomes. By repeatedly visualizing yourself overcoming challenges and achieving your goals, you program your mind for success and develop a strong belief in your abilities.

4. **Enhancing Problem-Solving Skills**: Visualization can also be used as a problem-solving tool. By visualizing different scenarios and outcomes, you can explore potential solutions and make more informed decisions.

2.4.2 How to Visualize Your Success

TO HARNESS THE POWER of visualization, follow these steps:

1. **Create a Quiet Space**: Find a quiet and comfortable space where you can relax and focus without distractions. This could be a quiet room in your home

or a peaceful outdoor setting.

2. **Relax Your Mind and Body**: Take a few deep breaths and consciously release any tension or stress in your body. Relax your mind by clearing your thoughts and focusing on the present moment.

3. **Set Clear Intentions**: Before you begin visualizing, set clear intentions about what you want to achieve. Be specific about your goals and outcomes, and visualize them as if they have already been accomplished.

4. **Engage Your Senses**: As you visualize, engage all your senses to make the experience more vivid and real. See the images, hear the sounds, and feel the emotions associated with your success.

5. **Repetition and Consistency**: Practice visualization regularly to reinforce your mental images and strengthen your belief in your ability to achieve your goals. The more you visualize, the more powerful the impact will be.

6. **Take Inspired Action**: Visualization alone is not enough. It is important to take inspired action towards your goals. Use your visualizations as a guide and take the necessary steps to turn your dreams into reality.

2.4.3 Visualization Techniques for Online Entrepreneurs

HERE ARE SOME VISUALIZATION techniques that can specifically benefit online entrepreneurs:

1. **Visualizing Your Ideal Online Business**: Close your eyes and imagine your ideal online business. Visualize the website, the products or services you offer, and the satisfied customers. See yourself managing your business with ease and enjoying the financial success that comes with it.

2. **Visualizing Successful Marketing Campaigns**: Picture yourself launching successful marketing campaigns that attract a large audience and generate high conversion rates. Visualize the positive feedback from customers and the growth of your online presence.

3. **Visualizing Positive Interactions with Customers**: Imagine yourself engaging with your target audience and providing exceptional customer service. Visualize positive interactions, satisfied customers, and glowing testimonials that contribute to the success of your online business.

4. **Visualizing Financial Abundance**: Create a mental image of financial abundance and prosperity. See yourself achieving your financial goals, paying off debts, and enjoying the freedom and flexibility that comes with financial success.

5. **Visualizing Personal and Professional Growth**: Visualize yourself continuously learning and growing as an online entrepreneur. See yourself acquiring new skills, expanding your knowledge, and becoming a recognized authority in your industry.

Remember, visualization is a tool that can enhance your mindset and propel you towards success. Combine it with action, perseverance, and a growth mindset, and you will be well on your way to achieving your goals as an online entrepreneur.

Visualization is a practice that successful entrepreneurs and individuals from various fields have used to manifest their dreams and create extraordinary results. Embrace the power of visualization and let it guide you on your journey to online entrepreneurial success.

BUILDING YOUR ONLINE Presence

3.1 Choosing the Right Platform

―――

I n today's digital age, having a strong online presence is crucial for the success of any business. One of the first steps in building your online presence is choosing the right platform. With so many options available, it can be overwhelming to determine which platform is best suited for your business. In this section, we will explore the factors to consider when choosing a platform and provide guidance on making an informed decision.

3.1.1 Understanding Your Business Needs

BEFORE DIVING INTO the world of online platforms, it is essential to have a clear understanding of your business needs. Consider the nature of your products or services, your target audience, and your long-term goals. Are you planning to sell physical products, digital goods, or services? Do you need a platform that supports e-commerce functionality? Understanding your business needs will help you narrow down your options and find a platform that aligns with your goals.

3.1.2 Evaluating Platform Features

DIFFERENT PLATFORMS offer various features and functionalities. It is important to evaluate these features and determine which ones are essential for your business. Some key features to consider include:

Ease of Use

CONSIDER THE PLATFORM'S user interface and how easy it is to navigate and manage. A user-friendly platform will save you time and effort in the long run.

Customization Options

LOOK FOR PLATFORMS that allow you to customize your website or online store to reflect your brand identity. The ability to personalize your platform will help you create a unique and memorable online presence.

Scalability

CONSIDER THE SCALABILITY of the platform. Will it be able to accommodate your business's growth and handle increased traffic and sales? It is important to choose a platform that can grow with your business.

Mobile Responsiveness

WITH THE INCREASING use of mobile devices, it is crucial to have a platform that is mobile-responsive. This ensures that your website or online store looks and functions well on smartphones and tablets.

SEO Capabilities

SEARCH ENGINE OPTIMIZATION (SEO) is vital for driving organic traffic to your website. Look for platforms that offer built-in SEO features or allow you to optimize your content for search engines.

Integration Options

CONSIDER THE PLATFORM'S integration capabilities. Can it integrate with other tools and software that you use for your business, such as email marketing platforms or customer relationship management (CRM) systems? Integration with other tools can streamline your business processes and improve efficiency.

3.1.3 Researching Platform Options

ONCE YOU HAVE A CLEAR understanding of your business needs and the features you require, it's time to research platform options. There are several popular platforms available, each with its own strengths and weaknesses. Some of the most common platforms include:

WordPress

WORDPRESS IS A VERSATILE platform that can be used for both blogging and building websites. It offers a wide range of themes and plugins, allowing for customization and flexibility. WordPress is a popular choice for content-based websites and blogs.

Shopify

SHOPIFY IS A LEADING e-commerce platform that specializes in creating online stores. It offers a user-friendly interface, a wide range of themes, and robust e-commerce features. Shopify is an excellent choice for businesses looking to sell physical or digital products online.

Wix

WIX IS A BEGINNER-FRIENDLY platform that offers drag-and-drop website building capabilities. It provides a variety of templates and customization options, making it easy to create a visually appealing website. Wix is suitable for small businesses and individuals looking for a simple and affordable solution.

Squarespace

SQUARESPACE IS KNOWN for its sleek and modern templates, making it a popular choice for creative professionals and businesses in the design industry. It offers a user-friendly interface and integrates well with other tools and software.

Magento

MAGENTO IS A ROBUST e-commerce platform that caters to businesses with complex needs. It offers advanced features and customization options, making it suitable for large-scale online stores. Magento requires technical expertise and is recommended for businesses with a dedicated development team.

3.1.4 Weighing the Pros and Cons

AFTER RESEARCHING DIFFERENT platform options, it's important to weigh the pros and cons of each platform based on your business needs and goals. Consider factors such as cost, ease of use, scalability, and the level of technical expertise required. It may be helpful to create a comparison chart or list to evaluate each platform objectively.

3.1.5 Seeking Recommendations and Reviews

IN ADDITION TO CONDUCTING your own research, it can be beneficial to seek recommendations and read reviews from other entrepreneurs who have used the platforms you are considering. Online forums, social media groups, and industry-specific communities are great places to connect with like-minded individuals and gather insights from their experiences.

3.1.6 Making an Informed Decision

CHOOSING THE RIGHT platform for your online business is a critical decision that can impact your success in the long run. By understanding your business needs, evaluating platform features, researching options, weighing the pros and cons, and seeking recommendations, you can make an informed decision that aligns with your goals and sets you up for success.

Remember, the choice of platform is not set in stone. As your business evolves, you may need to switch platforms or integrate additional tools and software. The key is to choose a platform that provides the foundation for your online presence and can adapt to your changing needs.

In the next section, we will explore the process of creating a professional website to establish your online presence and attract your target audience.

3.2 Creating a Professional Website

———

In today's digital age, having a professional website is essential for any online entrepreneur. Your website serves as the virtual storefront for your business, representing your brand and showcasing your products or services to potential customers. A well-designed and user-friendly website can significantly impact your online presence and contribute to the success of your business. In this section, we will explore the key elements of creating a professional website that effectively communicates your brand and engages your target audience.

3.2.1 Defining Your Website's Purpose

BEFORE DIVING INTO the technical aspects of website creation, it is crucial to define the purpose of your website. Ask yourself: What do you want to achieve with your website? Are you looking to sell products directly, generate leads, provide information, or build an online community? Understanding the primary purpose of your website will guide your design choices and content creation.

3.2.2 Choosing a Domain Name

A DOMAIN NAME IS THE web address that users will type into their browsers to access your website. It is important to choose a domain name that is memorable, relevant to your business, and easy to spell. Ideally, your domain name should reflect your brand and be aligned with your overall marketing strategy. Consider using keywords related to your industry to improve search engine optimization (SEO) and make it easier for potential customers to find you online.

3.2.3 Selecting a Website Platform

THERE ARE VARIOUS WEBSITE platforms available, each with its own set of features and customization options. Popular website builders like WordPress, Wix, and Squarespace offer user-friendly interfaces and templates that allow you to create a professional website without extensive coding knowledge. Research different platforms and choose one that aligns with your technical abilities and business requirements.

3.2.4 Designing Your Website

THE DESIGN OF YOUR website plays a crucial role in attracting and retaining visitors. A clean and visually appealing design will create a positive user experience and convey professionalism. Consider the following design elements:

3.2.4.1 Layout and Navigation

ENSURE THAT YOUR WEBSITE has a clear and intuitive layout that guides visitors through the different sections. Use a consistent navigation menu that is easily accessible and includes essential pages such as Home, About, Products/ Services, and Contact. Organize your content in a logical manner, making it easy for users to find the information they are looking for.

3.2.4.2 Branding and Visual Identity

YOUR WEBSITE SHOULD reflect your brand's visual identity, including your logo, color scheme, and typography. Consistency in branding across your website and other marketing materials will help build brand recognition and trust. Use high-quality images and graphics that are relevant to your business and resonate with your target audience.

3.2.4.3 Mobile Responsiveness

WITH THE INCREASING use of mobile devices, it is essential to ensure that your website is mobile-responsive. This means that your website adapts and displays properly on different screen sizes, providing a seamless user experience across devices. Test your website on various devices to ensure it is optimized for mobile viewing.

3.2.5 Creating Compelling Content

CONTENT IS KING WHEN it comes to engaging your website visitors and driving conversions. Develop high-quality and relevant content that aligns with your target audience's needs and interests. Consider the following content elements:

3.2.5.1 Homepage

YOUR HOMEPAGE IS THE first impression visitors will have of your website. It should clearly communicate your brand's value proposition and provide a glimpse into what your business offers. Use compelling headlines, concise copy, and visually appealing images or videos to capture visitors' attention and encourage them to explore further.

3.2.5.2 About Page

THE ABOUT PAGE IS AN opportunity to tell your brand's story and connect with your audience on a deeper level. Share information about your company's history, mission, values, and team members. Use this page to build trust and establish credibility with your visitors.

3.2.5.3 Product/Service Pages

IF YOU ARE SELLING products or services, create dedicated pages that provide detailed information about each offering. Include high-quality images, clear descriptions, pricing, and any other relevant details. Make it easy for visitors to make a purchase or inquire further.

3.2.5.4 Blog or Resource Center

A BLOG OR RESOURCE center can be a valuable addition to your website. Regularly publishing informative and engaging content related to your industry can position you as an authority and attract organic traffic from search engines. Use this platform to share valuable insights, tips, and industry news with your audience.

3.2.6 Optimizing for Search Engines

SEARCH ENGINE OPTIMIZATION (SEO) is the process of improving your website's visibility in search engine results. By optimizing your website for relevant keywords and implementing SEO best practices, you can increase organic traffic and attract potential customers. Consider the following SEO strategies:

3.2.6.1 Keyword Research

IDENTIFY RELEVANT KEYWORDS that your target audience is likely to search for when looking for products or services similar to yours. Use keyword research tools to discover high-volume and low-competition keywords that you can incorporate into your website's content.

3.2.6.2 On-Page Optimization

OPTIMIZE YOUR WEBSITE'S meta tags, headings, URLs, and image alt tags with relevant keywords. Ensure that your content is well-structured, easy to read, and provides value to your visitors. Aim to create comprehensive and informative content that answers your audience's questions.

3.2.6.3 Link Building

BUILDING HIGH-QUALITY backlinks from reputable websites can significantly improve your website's authority and search engine rankings. Seek opportunities to collaborate with influencers, guest post on relevant blogs, or participate in industry forums to earn valuable backlinks.

3.2.7 Ensuring Website Security

WEBSITE SECURITY IS of utmost importance to protect your business and your customers' data. Implement security measures such as SSL certificates, regular backups, and strong passwords to safeguard your website from potential threats. Regularly update your website's software and plugins to ensure they are secure and up to date.

3.2.8 Testing and Optimization

ONCE YOUR WEBSITE IS live, it is essential to continuously test and optimize its performance. Monitor website analytics to gain insights into user behavior, identify areas for improvement, and make data-driven decisions. Test different elements such as headlines, call-to-action buttons, and page layouts to optimize conversion rates and improve user experience.

Creating a professional website is a critical step in establishing your online presence and attracting customers. By defining your website's purpose, choosing the right platform, designing an appealing layout, creating compelling content, optimizing for search engines, ensuring security, and continuously testing and optimizing, you can create a website that effectively represents your brand and drives business growth.

3.3 Optimizing for Search Engines

In today's digital age, having a strong online presence is crucial for the success of any business. One of the most effective ways to increase your visibility and reach a wider audience is by optimizing your website for search engines. Search engine optimization (SEO) is the process of improving your website's visibility in search engine results pages (SERPs) through organic (non-paid) methods. By implementing SEO strategies, you can improve your website's ranking in search engine results, drive more organic traffic, and ultimately increase your chances of converting visitors into customers.

3.3.1 Understanding Search Engine Algorithms

BEFORE DIVING INTO the specifics of SEO, it's important to understand how search engines work. Search engines like Google, Bing, and Yahoo use complex algorithms to determine the relevance and quality of websites in relation to a user's search query. These algorithms take into account various factors such as keywords, website structure, user experience, and backlinks to determine the ranking of websites in search results.

Search engine algorithms are constantly evolving to provide users with the most relevant and high-quality search results. As an online entrepreneur, it's essential to stay updated with the latest algorithm changes and adapt your SEO strategies accordingly.

3.3.2 Keyword Research and Optimization

KEYWORDS ARE THE FOUNDATION of SEO. They are the words or phrases that users type into search engines when looking for information, products, or services. Conducting thorough keyword research is crucial to identify the keywords that are relevant to your business and have a high search volume.

Start by brainstorming a list of keywords that are relevant to your business. Put yourself in the shoes of your target audience and think about the words they would use to search for products or services similar to yours. Once you have a list of potential keywords, use keyword research tools like Google Keyword Planner, SEMrush, or Moz Keyword Explorer to analyze their search volume and competition level.

Once you have identified your target keywords, it's important to optimize your website's content accordingly. Incorporate your keywords naturally into your website's meta tags, headings, titles, and body content. However, avoid keyword stuffing, which is the practice of excessively using keywords in an attempt to manipulate search engine rankings. Search engines penalize websites that engage in keyword stuffing, so it's important to maintain a balance between optimization and providing valuable content to your users.

3.3.3 On-Page Optimization

ON-PAGE OPTIMIZATION refers to the optimization of individual web pages to improve their visibility in search engine results. It involves optimizing various elements on your website to make it more search engine-friendly.

One of the key elements of on-page optimization is optimizing your website's meta tags. Meta tags are snippets of HTML code that provide information about a web page to search engines. The two most important meta tags for SEO are the meta title and meta description. The meta title is the title of your web page that appears as the clickable headline in search engine results. The meta description is a brief summary of your web page's content that appears below the meta title in search engine results. Optimize your meta tags by incorporating relevant keywords and making them compelling to encourage users to click on your website.

Another important aspect of on-page optimization is optimizing your website's URL structure. Use descriptive and keyword-rich URLs that accurately reflect the content of your web pages. For example, instead of using a generic URL like "", use a descriptive URL like "". This not only helps search engines understand the content of your web pages but also makes it easier for users to navigate your website.

Additionally, optimize your website's headings by using header tags (H1, H2, H3, etc.) to structure your content. Use your target keywords in your headings to signal to search engines the relevance of your content. Also, ensure that your website's content is well-organized, easy to read, and provides valuable information to your users.

3.3.4 Off-Page Optimization

OFF-PAGE OPTIMIZATION refers to the actions taken outside of your website to improve its visibility and authority in search engine results. The most important aspect of off-page optimization is building high-quality backlinks to your website.

Backlinks are links from other websites that point to your website. Search engines consider backlinks as votes of confidence for your website's credibility and authority. The more high-quality backlinks you have, the higher your website is likely to rank in search engine results.

There are several strategies you can employ to build backlinks to your website. One effective strategy is to create high-quality, shareable content that naturally attracts backlinks from other websites. This can include blog posts, infographics, videos, or any other form of content that provides value to your target audience. Promote your content through social media, email marketing, and outreach to relevant websites or influencers in your industry to increase its visibility and encourage backlinks.

Another strategy is to actively seek out opportunities for guest blogging. Guest blogging involves writing and publishing articles on other websites in exchange for a backlink to your website. Look for reputable websites in your industry that accept guest posts and pitch them relevant and valuable content ideas.

It's important to note that when building backlinks, quality is more important than quantity. Focus on acquiring backlinks from authoritative and relevant websites rather than engaging in spammy link-building practices. Search engines can detect and penalize websites that engage in manipulative link-building tactics.

3.3.5 Monitoring and Analytics

ONCE YOU HAVE IMPLEMENTED SEO strategies on your website, it's important to monitor and analyze the results to determine the effectiveness of your efforts. Use web analytics tools like Google Analytics to track important metrics such as organic traffic, bounce rate, conversion rate, and keyword rankings.

Regularly review your website's analytics to identify areas for improvement and make data-driven decisions. Analyze the keywords that are driving the most traffic to your website and optimize your content further to target those keywords. Monitor your website's backlink profile to ensure that you are acquiring high-quality backlinks and disavow any spammy or low-quality backlinks that may harm your website's ranking.

By continuously monitoring and analyzing your website's performance, you can make informed decisions to optimize your SEO strategies and improve your website's visibility in search engine results.

Conclusion

OPTIMIZING YOUR WEBSITE for search engines is a critical component of building a successful online business. By understanding search engine algorithms, conducting thorough keyword research, implementing on-page and off-page optimization strategies, and monitoring your website's performance, you can improve your website's visibility, drive more organic traffic, and ultimately increase your chances of success in the competitive online landscape. Remember, SEO is an ongoing process, and it requires continuous effort and adaptation to stay ahead of the competition and maintain a strong online presence.

3.4 Leveraging Social Media

———

In today's digital age, social media has become an integral part of our lives. It has revolutionized the way we connect, communicate, and consume information. As an online entrepreneur, leveraging social media platforms can be a game-changer for your business. It provides you with a powerful tool to reach and engage with your target audience, build brand awareness, and drive traffic to your website. In this section, we will explore the strategies and best practices for effectively leveraging social media to grow your online presence and achieve your business goals.

3.4.1 Choosing the Right Social Media Platforms

WITH NUMEROUS SOCIAL media platforms available, it's essential to choose the ones that align with your target audience and business objectives. Each platform has its unique features, demographics, and user behavior. Here are some popular social media platforms and their key characteristics:

1. Facebook: With over 2.8 billion monthly active users, Facebook is the largest social media platform. It offers a wide range of features, including business pages, groups, and advertising options. It is suitable for businesses targeting a broad audience and looking to build brand awareness.
2. Instagram: Known for its visual content, Instagram is

popular among younger demographics. It is ideal for businesses in industries such as fashion, beauty, travel, and food. Instagram offers features like stories, IGTV, and shopping tags, enabling businesses to showcase their products or services creatively.

3. Twitter: Twitter is a microblogging platform that allows users to share short messages called tweets. It is known for its real-time updates and conversations. Twitter is suitable for businesses looking to engage with their audience, share news and updates, and participate in industry discussions.

4. LinkedIn: LinkedIn is a professional networking platform primarily used for business and career-related purposes. It is ideal for B2B businesses, professionals, and entrepreneurs looking to establish thought leadership, network, and generate leads.

5. YouTube: As the second-largest search engine after Google, YouTube is a video-sharing platform with billions of users. It is suitable for businesses that can create engaging video content to educate, entertain, or demonstrate their products or services.

When choosing social media platforms, consider your target audience's demographics, interests, and preferred platforms. It's better to focus on a few platforms and maintain an active presence rather than spreading yourself too thin across multiple platforms.

3.4.2 Developing a Social Media Strategy

TO EFFECTIVELY LEVERAGE social media, it's crucial to have a well-defined strategy in place. A social media strategy outlines your goals, target audience, content plan, and engagement tactics. Here are some key steps to develop a social media strategy:

1. Set Clear Goals: Define what you want to achieve through social media. It could be increasing brand awareness, driving website traffic, generating leads, or improving customer engagement. Ensure your goals are specific, measurable, attainable, relevant, and time-bound (SMART).

2. Identify Your Target Audience: Understand your target audience's demographics, interests, and pain points. This knowledge will help you create content that resonates with them and tailor your messaging accordingly.

3. Choose the Right Content Mix: Determine the types of content you will share on social media. It could include blog posts, videos, infographics, user-generated content, or industry news. Experiment with different formats to see what resonates best with your audience.

4. Create a Content Calendar: Plan your social media content in advance using a content calendar. This ensures a consistent posting schedule and helps you stay organized. Consider using social media management tools to schedule and automate your posts.

5. Engage and Interact: Social media is not just about broadcasting your message; it's also about building relationships. Engage with your audience by responding to comments, messages, and mentions. Participate in relevant conversations and join industry-specific groups or communities.

6. Monitor and Analyze: Regularly monitor your social media performance using analytics tools provided by each platform or third-party tools. Analyze metrics such as reach, engagement, click-through rates, and conversions. Use these insights to refine your strategy and optimize your content.

Remember, social media success doesn't happen overnight. It requires consistency, experimentation, and continuous improvement. Be patient and adapt your strategy based on the feedback and data you gather.

3.4.3 Paid Advertising on Social Media

WHILE ORGANIC REACH on social media has declined over the years, paid advertising offers a way to amplify your reach and target specific audiences. Social media platforms provide robust advertising options to help you achieve your business objectives. Here are some common types of social media advertising:

1. Facebook Ads: Facebook offers a wide range of ad formats, including image ads, video ads, carousel ads, and lead generation ads. You can target specific demographics, interests, behaviors, and even retarget

website visitors.

2. Instagram Ads: Instagram ads appear in users' feeds or stories. You can create visually appealing ads that blend seamlessly with organic content. Instagram also offers shopping tags, allowing users to purchase products directly from the platform.

3. Twitter Ads: Twitter offers various ad formats, including promoted tweets, promoted accounts, and promoted trends. You can target specific keywords, interests, or demographics to reach your desired audience.

4. LinkedIn Ads: LinkedIn ads allow you to target professionals based on their job titles, industries, or company size. You can create sponsored content, text ads, or dynamic ads to promote your products or services.

When running paid social media campaigns, it's essential to define your target audience, set a budget, and monitor your campaign's performance. Regularly analyze the data and make adjustments to optimize your ads for better results.

3.4.4 Influencer Marketing

INFLUENCER MARKETING has gained significant popularity in recent years. It involves collaborating with influential individuals on social media to promote your products or services. Influencers have a loyal following and can help you reach a wider audience. Here are some steps to leverage influencer marketing:

1. Identify Relevant Influencers: Research and identify influencers who align with your brand values, target audience, and industry. Look for influencers with an engaged and authentic following.
2. Establish Relationships: Reach out to influencers and build relationships with them. Engage with their content, comment on their posts, and share their content. This helps create a connection and increases the likelihood of them collaborating with you.
3. Define Collaboration Terms: Clearly define the terms of the collaboration, including the type of content, deliverables, timeline, and compensation. Ensure both parties are aligned on expectations and goals.
4. Track and Measure Results: Monitor the performance of influencer campaigns using unique tracking links, promo codes, or affiliate programs. Measure the impact on brand awareness, website traffic, conversions, or sales.

Influencer marketing can be a powerful way to leverage social media and tap into the influencer's credibility and reach. However, it's essential to choose influencers carefully and ensure their values align with your brand.

3.4.5 Social Media Best Practices

TO MAKE THE MOST OF social media, here are some best practices to keep in mind:

1. Consistency: Maintain a consistent posting schedule to keep your audience engaged. Experiment with

different posting frequencies and times to find what works best for your audience.

2. Quality Content: Focus on creating high-quality, valuable content that resonates with your audience. Use a mix of educational, entertaining, and promotional content to keep your audience engaged.

3. Visual Appeal: Use visually appealing images, videos, and graphics to capture your audience's attention. Invest in professional photography or graphic design if necessary.

4. Engage and Respond: Actively engage with your audience by responding to comments, messages, and mentions. Show appreciation for positive feedback and address any concerns or complaints promptly.

5. Stay Up-to-Date: Social media platforms are constantly evolving. Stay informed about new features, algorithm changes, and best practices to adapt your strategy accordingly.

6. Test and Iterate: Social media is a dynamic landscape. Continuously test different content formats, messaging, and strategies. Analyze the results and make data-driven decisions to optimize your social media efforts.

By leveraging social media effectively, you can build a strong online presence, connect with your target audience, and drive meaningful business results. Embrace the power of social media and unlock the potential for your online entrepreneurship journey.

3.5 Engaging with Your Target Audience

———

E ngaging with your target audience is a crucial aspect of building a successful online business. It involves creating meaningful connections, fostering relationships, and understanding the needs and preferences of your customers. By engaging with your target audience, you can build trust, loyalty, and a strong brand reputation. In this section, we will explore various strategies and techniques to effectively engage with your target audience and create a thriving online community.

3.5.1 Understanding Your Target Audience

BEFORE YOU CAN ENGAGE with your target audience, it is essential to have a deep understanding of who they are. Conducting market research and creating buyer personas can help you gain valuable insights into the demographics, interests, and behaviors of your target audience. By understanding their needs, pain points, and aspirations, you can tailor your marketing messages and content to resonate with them.

3.5.2 Creating Compelling Content

ONE OF THE MOST EFFECTIVE ways to engage with your target audience is through compelling content. Whether it's blog posts, videos, podcasts, or social media updates, creating high-quality and valuable content is key to capturing the attention and interest of your audience. Your content should be informative, entertaining, and relevant to your target audience's interests and needs. By consistently delivering valuable content, you can establish yourself as an authority in your niche and build a loyal following.

3.5.3 Utilizing Social Media Platforms

SOCIAL MEDIA PLATFORMS provide a powerful avenue for engaging with your target audience. With billions of active users, platforms like Facebook, Instagram, Twitter, and LinkedIn offer immense opportunities to connect with your audience on a personal level. By sharing engaging content, responding to comments and messages, and actively participating in relevant communities and groups, you can build a strong online presence and foster meaningful relationships with your audience.

3.5.4 Hosting Webinars and Live Events

WEBINARS AND LIVE EVENTS are excellent ways to engage with your target audience in real-time. These interactive platforms allow you to share your expertise, answer questions, and provide valuable insights to your audience. By hosting webinars and live events, you can establish yourself as a thought leader in your industry and create a sense of community among your audience. Additionally, these events provide an opportunity for direct interaction and feedback, allowing you to better understand your audience's needs and preferences.

3.5.5 Encouraging User-generated Content

USER-GENERATED CONTENT is a powerful tool for engaging with your target audience. By encouraging your audience to create and share content related to your brand, you can foster a sense of community and increase brand loyalty. User-generated content can take various forms, such as testimonials, reviews, social media posts, and blog articles. By showcasing and acknowledging user-generated content, you not only engage with your audience but also leverage their influence to reach a wider audience.

3.5.6 Personalizing Communication

PERSONALIZATION IS key to effective audience engagement. By tailoring your communication and marketing messages to individual customers, you can create a more personalized and meaningful experience. Utilize customer data and segmentation to deliver targeted messages, offers, and recommendations. Personalization can be achieved through email marketing, personalized landing pages, and dynamic content that adapts to the preferences and behaviors of your audience.

3.5.7 Actively Listening and Responding

ENGAGING WITH YOUR target audience is a two-way process. It is essential to actively listen to your audience's feedback, comments, and concerns and respond in a timely and meaningful manner. By demonstrating that you value their opinions and are responsive to their needs, you can build trust and loyalty. Actively monitoring social media channels, email inboxes, and customer feedback platforms allows you to address any issues promptly and provide exceptional customer service.

3.5.8 Building Online Communities

BUILDING AN ONLINE community is a powerful way to engage with your target audience. By creating a space where like-minded individuals can connect, share ideas, and support each other, you can foster a sense of belonging and loyalty. Online communities can take various forms, such as forums, Facebook groups, or membership sites. By actively participating in these communities, providing valuable content, and facilitating discussions, you can establish yourself as a trusted authority and create a thriving community around your brand.

3.5.9 Analyzing and Adapting

ENGAGING WITH YOUR target audience is an ongoing process that requires continuous analysis and adaptation. By monitoring and analyzing data, such as website analytics, social media metrics, and customer feedback, you can gain valuable insights into the effectiveness of your engagement strategies. Use this data to identify areas for improvement, experiment with new approaches, and refine your engagement tactics. By staying agile and responsive to your audience's needs, you can continuously enhance your engagement efforts and build stronger relationships with your target audience.

Engaging with your target audience is a dynamic and iterative process. It requires a deep understanding of your audience, the creation of compelling content, active participation in social media platforms, hosting webinars and live events, encouraging user-generated content, personalizing communication, actively listening and responding, building online communities, and continuously analyzing and adapting your strategies. By implementing these strategies, you can create a thriving online community, build strong relationships with your target audience, and drive the success of your online business.

Digital Marketing Strategies

4.1 Understanding Digital Marketing Channels

═══

In today's digital age, understanding and utilizing digital marketing channels is essential for the success of any online business. Digital marketing channels refer to the various platforms and strategies that businesses use to promote their products or services online. These channels provide opportunities to reach a wider audience, increase brand visibility, and drive targeted traffic to your website. In this section, we will explore the different digital marketing channels available and how you can leverage them to grow your online business.

4.1.1 Search Engine Optimization (SEO)

SEARCH ENGINE OPTIMIZATION, or SEO, is the process of optimizing your website to rank higher in search engine results pages (SERPs). When users search for keywords related to your business, you want your website to appear at the top of the search results. This is important because higher rankings lead to increased visibility and organic traffic.

To improve your website's SEO, you need to focus on several key factors. First, you should conduct keyword research to identify the keywords that your target audience is searching for. Once you have identified these keywords, you can optimize your website's content by incorporating them naturally into your website's pages, titles, headings, and meta descriptions.

Additionally, you should ensure that your website is user-friendly and easy to navigate. Search engines prioritize websites that provide a positive user experience. This includes having a fast loading speed, mobile responsiveness, and clear site structure.

Another important aspect of SEO is building high-quality backlinks. Backlinks are links from other websites that point to your website. Search engines consider backlinks as a vote of confidence in your website's credibility and authority. You can build backlinks by creating valuable content that other websites will want to link to, guest posting on relevant blogs, and engaging with influencers in your industry.

4.1.2 Pay-Per-Click Advertising (PPC)

PAY-PER-CLICK ADVERTISING, or PPC, is a digital marketing strategy where advertisers pay a fee each time their ad is clicked. This form of advertising allows businesses to display their ads on search engine results pages, social media platforms, and other websites. PPC is an effective way to drive targeted traffic to your website and increase conversions.

The most popular PPC platform is Google Ads, which allows businesses to create ads that appear on Google's search results pages. With Google Ads, you can target specific keywords and demographics to ensure that your ads are shown to the right audience. Facebook Ads is another popular PPC platform that allows businesses to target users based on their interests, demographics, and behaviors.

To run successful PPC campaigns, it is important to conduct thorough keyword research and create compelling ad copy. Your ads should be relevant to the keywords you are targeting and should include a clear call-to-action. It is also important to continuously monitor and optimize your campaigns to ensure that you are getting the best return on investment (ROI).

4.1.3 Social Media Marketing

SOCIAL MEDIA MARKETING involves using social media platforms such as Facebook, Instagram, Twitter, and LinkedIn to promote your products or services. Social media platforms provide a unique opportunity to engage with your target audience, build brand awareness, and drive traffic to your website.

To effectively utilize social media marketing, you need to identify the platforms that are most relevant to your target audience. Each platform has its own demographics and user behavior, so it is important to choose the platforms where your target audience is most active. Once you have identified the platforms, you can create a social media strategy that includes regular posting, engaging with your audience, and running targeted ad campaigns.

When creating content for social media, it is important to provide value to your audience. This can include sharing informative articles, creating engaging videos, or hosting live Q&A sessions. By providing valuable content, you can build trust and credibility with your audience, which can lead to increased brand loyalty and customer retention.

4.1.4 Content Marketing

CONTENT MARKETING IS a strategic approach to creating and distributing valuable, relevant, and consistent content to attract and retain a clearly defined audience. Content can take various forms, including blog posts, videos, podcasts, infographics, and ebooks. The goal of content marketing is to provide valuable information to your audience while subtly promoting your products or services.

To develop a successful content marketing strategy, you need to understand your target audience and their needs. By conducting market research and creating buyer personas, you can identify the topics and formats that resonate with your audience. Your content should be informative, engaging, and shareable, and it should align with your brand's values and messaging.

In addition to creating high-quality content, it is important to promote your content through various channels. This can include sharing your content on social media, reaching out to influencers for collaborations, and optimizing your content for search engines. By promoting your content effectively, you can increase its reach and attract a larger audience to your website.

4.1.5 Email Marketing

EMAIL MARKETING IS a powerful tool for building relationships with your audience and driving conversions. It involves sending targeted emails to your subscribers with the goal of nurturing leads, promoting products or services, and driving traffic to your website.

To effectively utilize email marketing, you need to build a quality email list. This can be done by offering valuable content or incentives in exchange for email addresses. Once you have a list of subscribers, you can segment them based on their interests, demographics, or purchase history to ensure that your emails are relevant and personalized.

When creating email campaigns, it is important to provide value to your subscribers. This can include sharing exclusive content, offering discounts or promotions, or providing helpful tips and advice. Your emails should be visually appealing, mobile-friendly, and include clear call-to-action buttons.

To measure the success of your email campaigns, you should track key metrics such as open rates, click-through rates, and conversion rates. This data can help you optimize your campaigns and improve your overall email marketing strategy.

By understanding and utilizing these digital marketing channels, you can effectively promote your online business, reach your target audience, and drive growth and success. Each channel has its own unique advantages and strategies, so it is important to experiment and find the mix that works best for your business. Remember to continuously monitor and optimize your marketing efforts to ensure that you are maximizing your return on investment and achieving your business goals.

4.2 Developing a Content Marketing Strategy

―――

I n today's digital age, content marketing has become an essential component of any successful online business. It is a strategic approach that involves creating and distributing valuable, relevant, and consistent content to attract and engage a target audience. A well-developed content marketing strategy can help you establish your brand, build trust with your audience, and drive traffic to your website. In this section, we will explore the key elements of developing an effective content marketing strategy.

4.2.1 Defining Your Target Audience

BEFORE YOU START CREATING content, it is crucial to have a clear understanding of your target audience. Who are they? What are their needs, interests, and pain points? By defining your target audience, you can tailor your content to resonate with them and provide value. Conduct market research, analyze your competitors, and gather insights from your existing customers to develop buyer personas that represent your ideal customers. These personas will serve as a guide for creating content that speaks directly to your audience's needs and desires.

4.2.2 Setting Clear Objectives

TO ENSURE THE SUCCESS of your content marketing efforts, it is essential to set clear objectives. What do you want to achieve with your content? Do you want to increase brand awareness, generate leads, drive website traffic, or establish thought leadership? Setting specific, measurable, achievable, relevant, and time-bound (SMART) goals will help you stay focused and track your progress. Your objectives will shape the type of content you create, the platforms you use, and the metrics you measure.

4.2.3 Creating Engaging and Valuable Content

THE HEART OF ANY CONTENT marketing strategy is creating high-quality, engaging, and valuable content. Your content should provide solutions to your audience's problems, answer their questions, and offer insights and expertise. It should be informative, entertaining, and shareable. Consider using a mix of different content formats such as blog posts, videos, infographics, podcasts, and ebooks to cater to different preferences and capture the attention of your audience. Remember to optimize your content for search engines by incorporating relevant keywords and providing meta descriptions.

4.2.4 Developing a Content Calendar

CONSISTENCY IS KEY when it comes to content marketing. Developing a content calendar will help you stay organized and ensure a steady flow of content. Plan your content in advance, taking into account important dates, events, and industry trends. A content calendar will also help you maintain a consistent brand voice and tone across all your content. It allows you to schedule and automate your content distribution, ensuring that your audience receives fresh and relevant content regularly.

4.2.5 Promoting Your Content

CREATING GREAT CONTENT is only half the battle. To maximize its reach and impact, you need to promote it effectively. Utilize various channels to distribute your content, such as social media platforms, email newsletters, guest blogging, and influencer collaborations. Engage with your audience by responding to comments, encouraging shares and likes, and participating in relevant online communities. Consider investing in paid advertising to amplify your content's reach and target specific demographics. Monitor the performance of your content and make adjustments based on the data and feedback you receive.

4.2.6 Measuring and Analyzing Results

TO EVALUATE THE EFFECTIVENESS of your content marketing strategy, it is crucial to measure and analyze your results. Identify key performance indicators (KPIs) that align with your objectives, such as website traffic, engagement metrics, lead generation, and conversion rates. Utilize analytics tools to track and measure these metrics, and regularly review and analyze the data to gain insights into what is working and what needs improvement. Use these insights to refine your content strategy and optimize your future content creation efforts.

4.2.7 Adapting and Evolving Your Strategy

THE DIGITAL LANDSCAPE is constantly evolving, and so should your content marketing strategy. Stay updated with industry trends, changes in consumer behavior, and emerging technologies. Continuously monitor and evaluate the performance of your content, and be willing to adapt and experiment with new approaches. Seek feedback from your audience and use it to refine your content and better meet their needs. By staying agile and responsive, you can ensure that your content marketing strategy remains effective and relevant in a rapidly changing online environment.

Developing a content marketing strategy is a continuous process that requires creativity, research, and analysis. By understanding your target audience, setting clear objectives, creating valuable content, promoting it effectively, and measuring your results, you can build a strong foundation for your online business and establish a meaningful connection with your audience. Remember, content is king in the digital world, and a well-executed content marketing strategy can be the key to your online entrepreneurial success.

4.3 Harnessing the Power of Email Marketing

———

E mail marketing is a powerful tool that allows online entrepreneurs to connect with their audience, build relationships, and drive conversions. In an era where social media platforms dominate the digital landscape, email marketing remains a highly effective strategy for reaching and engaging with potential customers. In this section, we will explore the various aspects of email marketing and how you can harness its power to grow your online business.

4.3.1 Building an Email List

THE FOUNDATION OF SUCCESSFUL email marketing lies in building a quality email list. Your email list consists of individuals who have willingly provided their email addresses and expressed interest in your products or services. These individuals are more likely to engage with your emails and convert into paying customers.

To build an email list, you need to offer something of value in exchange for your audience's email addresses. This can be in the form of a free e-book, a discount code, or exclusive access to premium content. By providing something valuable, you incentivize your audience to join your email list and establish a mutually beneficial relationship.

There are several strategies you can employ to grow your email list:

1. Opt-in forms: Place opt-in forms strategically on your website, landing pages, and blog posts to capture email addresses. Make sure the forms are visually appealing and clearly communicate the value of subscribing to your email list.

2. Lead magnets: Create compelling lead magnets that provide valuable information or resources to your audience. This could be a comprehensive guide, a checklist, or a video tutorial. Promote these lead magnets across your online platforms to attract potential subscribers.

3. Content upgrades: Offer additional content upgrades within your blog posts or articles. These upgrades provide extra value to your readers and encourage them to subscribe to your email list to access the bonus content.

4. Social media promotions: Leverage your social media presence to promote your email list. Create engaging posts that highlight the benefits of subscribing and direct your followers to your opt-in forms.

Remember, building an email list takes time and effort. Focus on attracting quality subscribers who are genuinely interested in your offerings rather than simply aiming for a large number of email addresses.

4.3.2 Crafting Compelling Email Content

ONCE YOU HAVE BUILT your email list, it's crucial to create compelling email content that engages your subscribers and drives action. Here are some key elements to consider when crafting your email content:

1. Personalization: Address your subscribers by their names and tailor your content to their specific interests and preferences. Personalization helps create a sense of connection and makes your emails more relevant and engaging.

2. Clear and concise messaging: Keep your emails concise and to the point. Use clear and compelling subject lines to grab your subscribers' attention and entice them to open your emails. Within the email, use short paragraphs, bullet points, and subheadings to make your content easily scannable.

3. Value-driven content: Provide value to your subscribers in every email you send. This can be in the form of educational content, exclusive offers, or insider tips. By consistently delivering value, you build trust and establish yourself as an authority in your niche.

4. Call-to-action: Every email should have a clear call-to-action (CTA) that directs your subscribers to take the desired action. Whether it's making a purchase, signing up for a webinar, or downloading a resource, your CTA should be compelling and easy to follow.

5. A/B testing: Experiment with different elements of your email content, such as subject lines, CTAs, and

email layouts. Conduct A/B tests to determine what resonates best with your audience and optimize your email campaigns accordingly.

4.3.3 Automating Email Campaigns

EMAIL AUTOMATION ALLOWS you to streamline your email marketing efforts and deliver targeted messages to your subscribers at the right time. By automating your email campaigns, you can nurture leads, onboard new customers, and re-engage inactive subscribers without manual intervention.

Here are some key automation strategies to consider:

1. Welcome series: Set up a series of automated emails to welcome new subscribers and introduce them to your brand. Use this opportunity to provide valuable information, showcase your products or services, and encourage engagement.
2. Drip campaigns: Create automated drip campaigns that deliver a series of emails over a specific period. Drip campaigns can be used to educate your subscribers, promote new products or services, or nurture leads through the sales funnel.
3. Abandoned cart emails: If a subscriber adds items to their cart but doesn't complete the purchase, send automated abandoned cart emails to remind them and offer incentives to complete the transaction.
4. Re-engagement campaigns: Identify inactive subscribers and send automated re-engagement emails to win them back. Offer exclusive discounts,

personalized recommendations, or valuable content to reignite their interest in your brand.

Email automation not only saves you time but also ensures that your subscribers receive relevant and timely messages, increasing the chances of conversion and customer retention.

4.3.4 Analyzing and Optimizing Email Campaigns

TO MAXIMIZE THE EFFECTIVENESS of your email marketing efforts, it's essential to analyze and optimize your email campaigns. By monitoring key metrics and making data-driven decisions, you can continuously improve your email marketing strategy.

Here are some metrics to track and analyze:

1. Open rate: The percentage of subscribers who open your emails. A low open rate may indicate that your subject lines are not compelling enough or that your emails are ending up in spam folders.
2. Click-through rate (CTR): The percentage of subscribers who click on links within your emails. A low CTR may indicate that your content or CTAs are not engaging enough.
3. Conversion rate: The percentage of subscribers who take the desired action, such as making a purchase or signing up for a webinar. Tracking conversion rates helps you assess the effectiveness of your email campaigns in driving desired outcomes.
4. Unsubscribe rate: The percentage of subscribers who

opt-out of your email list. A high unsubscribe rate may indicate that your content is not meeting your subscribers' expectations or that you are sending too many emails.

Use the insights gained from analyzing these metrics to optimize your email campaigns. Experiment with different subject lines, content formats, and CTAs to improve open rates, CTRs, and conversions. Continuously test and refine your email marketing strategy to achieve better results over time.

Harnessing the power of email marketing can significantly impact the growth and success of your online business. By building a quality email list, crafting compelling email content, automating your campaigns, and analyzing the results, you can effectively engage with your audience, nurture leads, and drive conversions. Embrace email marketing as a core component of your digital marketing strategy and unlock its potential to propel your online venture to new heights.

4.4 Utilizing Social Media Advertising

———

In today's digital age, social media has become an integral part of our lives. It has revolutionized the way we connect, communicate, and consume information. As an online entrepreneur, harnessing the power of social media advertising can be a game-changer for your business. It allows you to reach a wider audience, engage with potential customers, and drive targeted traffic to your website or online store. In this section, we will explore the strategies and best practices for utilizing social media advertising to maximize your online business's success.

4.4.1 Understanding the Importance of Social Media Advertising

SOCIAL MEDIA PLATFORMS such as Facebook, Instagram, Twitter, and LinkedIn have billions of active users worldwide. These platforms offer a unique opportunity for online entrepreneurs to connect with their target audience on a personal level. Social media advertising allows you to create highly targeted campaigns based on demographics, interests, and behaviors, ensuring that your message reaches the right people at the right time.

One of the key advantages of social media advertising is its cost-effectiveness. Compared to traditional advertising channels, social media advertising offers a higher return on investment (ROI) and allows you to reach a larger audience with a smaller budget. Additionally, social media platforms provide robust analytics and tracking tools, enabling you to measure the performance of your campaigns and make data-driven decisions.

4.4.2 Choosing the Right Social Media Platforms

WITH NUMEROUS SOCIAL media platforms available, it's essential to choose the ones that align with your target audience and business objectives. Each platform has its unique features, demographics, and user behavior. Here are some popular social media platforms and their key characteristics:

• Facebook: With over 2.8 billion monthly active users, Facebook is the largest social media platform. It offers a wide range of advertising options, including feed ads, carousel ads, and video ads. Facebook's targeting capabilities are highly advanced, allowing you to reach specific demographics, interests, and behaviors.

• Instagram: As a visually-driven platform, Instagram is ideal for businesses that have visually appealing products or services. It offers various ad formats, including photo ads, video ads, and stories ads. Instagram's user base is predominantly younger, making it an excellent platform for targeting millennials and Gen Z.

• Twitter: Known for its real-time updates and concise messaging, Twitter is a platform for engaging in conversations and sharing news. Twitter ads can be effective for promoting time-sensitive offers, events, or driving engagement with your brand.

• LinkedIn: If your business targets professionals or B2B customers, LinkedIn is the go-to platform. It offers advertising options such as sponsored content, sponsored InMail, and text ads. LinkedIn's targeting options focus on professional attributes such as job title, industry, and company size.

• YouTube: As the second-largest search engine after Google, YouTube provides an excellent opportunity for video advertising. YouTube ads can be displayed before, during, or after videos, allowing you to reach a vast audience.

When selecting social media platforms, consider your target audience's demographics, interests, and behavior. It's crucial to focus on platforms where your audience is most active and engaged.

4.4.3 Creating Compelling Social Media Ads

TO MAKE YOUR SOCIAL media ads stand out and capture the attention of your target audience, it's essential to create compelling and visually appealing content. Here are some tips for creating effective social media ads:

1. Define your objective: Clearly define the goal of your ad campaign. Whether it's driving website traffic, generating leads, or increasing brand awareness, having a clear objective will help you create focused and impactful ads.
2. Use eye-catching visuals: Visual content is key to

grabbing attention on social media. Use high-quality images or videos that are relevant to your brand and message. Ensure that your visuals are visually appealing, clear, and easy to understand.

3. Craft compelling copy: Write concise and persuasive copy that communicates the value proposition of your product or service. Use clear and compelling language to entice your audience to take action.

4. Incorporate a strong call-to-action (CTA): A strong CTA tells your audience what action you want them to take. Whether it's "Shop Now," "Sign Up," or "Learn More," make sure your CTA is clear, visible, and compelling.

5. Test and optimize: Social media advertising provides robust analytics and tracking tools. Continuously monitor the performance of your ads and make data-driven decisions. Test different ad formats, visuals, copy, and CTAs to optimize your campaigns for better results.

4.4.4 Targeting and Retargeting Strategies

ONE OF THE SIGNIFICANT advantages of social media advertising is the ability to target specific audiences based on demographics, interests, and behaviors. Here are some targeting and retargeting strategies to maximize the effectiveness of your social media ads:

1. Demographic targeting: Define your target audience based on demographics such as age, gender, location, and language. This ensures that your ads are shown to

the most relevant audience.

2. Interest-based targeting: Target users based on their interests, hobbies, and preferences. This allows you to reach people who are more likely to be interested in your products or services.

3. Lookalike audience targeting: Create lookalike audiences based on your existing customer base or website visitors. Social media platforms analyze the characteristics of your existing audience and find similar users who are likely to be interested in your business.

4. Retargeting: Retargeting allows you to reach users who have previously interacted with your website or social media profiles. By showing ads to users who have already shown interest in your brand, you can increase the chances of conversion.

5. Custom audience targeting: Upload your customer email list or create custom audiences based on specific criteria. This enables you to target your existing customers or reach users who have engaged with your brand in the past.

By utilizing these targeting and retargeting strategies, you can ensure that your social media ads are shown to the most relevant audience, increasing the chances of conversion and maximizing your ROI.

4.4.5 Monitoring and Optimizing Social Media Ad Campaigns

ONCE YOUR SOCIAL MEDIA ad campaigns are live, it's crucial to monitor their performance and make necessary optimizations. Here are some key metrics to track and optimize:

1. Click-through rate (CTR): CTR measures the percentage of users who clicked on your ad. A high CTR indicates that your ad is engaging and relevant to your audience.

2. Conversion rate: Conversion rate measures the percentage of users who completed a desired action, such as making a purchase or signing up for a newsletter. Optimizing your ad campaigns to increase the conversion rate is crucial for driving business growth.

3. Cost per click (CPC) or cost per acquisition (CPA): These metrics measure the cost of acquiring a click or a conversion. Monitoring and optimizing these metrics can help you maximize your ad budget and improve ROI.

4. Ad frequency: Ad frequency measures how often your ad is shown to the same user. It's essential to monitor ad frequency to avoid ad fatigue and ensure that your ads remain effective.

5. A/B testing: A/B testing involves creating multiple versions of your ads and testing them against each other to determine which performs better. Test different visuals, copy, CTAs, and targeting options to

optimize your campaigns.

By continuously monitoring and optimizing your social media ad campaigns, you can improve their performance, reach a wider audience, and drive better results for your online business.

Utilizing social media advertising is a powerful tool for online entrepreneurs to reach their target audience, drive traffic, and increase conversions. By understanding the importance of social media advertising, choosing the right platforms, creating compelling ads, targeting and retargeting effectively, and monitoring and optimizing campaigns, you can leverage the full potential of social media to grow your online business. Embrace the power of social media advertising and propel your online entrepreneurship journey to new heights of success.

Financial Intelligence for Online Entrepreneurs

5.1 Managing Business Finances

———

As an online entrepreneur, managing your business finances is crucial for the success and sustainability of your venture. Effective financial management allows you to make informed decisions, allocate resources wisely, and ensure profitability. In this section, we will explore key strategies and practices to help you effectively manage your business finances.

5.1.1 Tracking Income and Expenses

ONE OF THE FIRST STEPS in managing your business finances is to track your income and expenses. This involves keeping a record of all the money coming into your business (revenue) and all the money going out (expenses). By diligently tracking your income and expenses, you gain a clear understanding of your financial position and can make informed decisions about your business.

There are various tools and software available that can help you track your income and expenses efficiently. Consider using accounting software or online platforms that allow you to categorize and track your financial transactions. This will not only save you time but also provide you with accurate and up-to-date financial information.

5.1.2 Creating a Budget

CREATING A BUDGET IS an essential part of managing your business finances. A budget helps you plan and allocate your financial resources effectively. It allows you to set financial goals, control spending, and make strategic decisions about investments and expenses.

Start by identifying your fixed expenses, such as rent, utilities, and software subscriptions. Then, consider your variable expenses, such as marketing costs, inventory, and employee wages. By categorizing your expenses, you can prioritize and allocate funds accordingly.

When creating a budget, it's important to be realistic and consider both short-term and long-term financial goals. Regularly review and update your budget to reflect changes in your business and industry.

5.1.3 Cash Flow Management

CASH FLOW MANAGEMENT is crucial for the financial health of your online business. It involves monitoring the inflow and outflow of cash to ensure that you have enough funds to cover your expenses and obligations.

To effectively manage your cash flow, consider the following practices:

1. **Monitor and project cash flow:** Regularly review your cash flow statement to understand your business's cash position. Project future cash flow based

on your sales forecasts and anticipated expenses.

2. **Manage accounts receivable:** Implement strategies to ensure timely payment from your customers. Offer incentives for early payment and establish clear payment terms and policies.

3. **Negotiate favorable payment terms:** When dealing with suppliers and vendors, negotiate payment terms that align with your cash flow needs. Consider options such as extended payment terms or discounts for early payment.

4. **Control expenses:** Regularly review your expenses and identify areas where you can reduce costs. Look for opportunities to negotiate better deals with suppliers or find more cost-effective alternatives.

5. **Maintain a cash reserve:** Set aside a portion of your revenue as a cash reserve to cover unexpected expenses or periods of low cash flow. This provides a safety net and ensures your business can continue operating smoothly.

5.1.4 Pricing Strategies and Profitability

SETTING THE RIGHT PRICES for your products or services is essential for profitability. Pricing too low may lead to financial losses, while pricing too high may deter potential customers. It's important to find the right balance that maximizes revenue and ensures profitability.

Consider the following factors when determining your pricing strategy:

1. **Costs:** Calculate all the costs associated with producing and delivering your products or services. This includes direct costs (materials, labor) and indirect costs (overhead, marketing).

2. **Competitor analysis:** Research your competitors' pricing strategies to understand the market landscape. Consider how your offering compares in terms of quality, features, and value.

3. **Value proposition:** Determine the unique value your products or services offer to customers. Price accordingly to reflect the perceived value and benefits.

4. **Pricing models:** Explore different pricing models, such as cost-plus pricing, value-based pricing, or subscription-based pricing. Choose a model that aligns with your business goals and target market.

5. **Regularly review and adjust:** Monitor your pricing strategy regularly and make adjustments as needed. Consider factors such as changes in costs, market demand, or competitive landscape.

5.1.5 Investing in Growth and Expansion

AS YOUR ONLINE BUSINESS grows, it's important to allocate resources strategically to fuel further growth and expansion. This may involve investing in new technologies, marketing campaigns, hiring additional staff, or expanding your product line.

When considering investments, evaluate the potential return on investment (ROI) and the impact on your business's financial health. Conduct thorough research and analysis to ensure that the investment aligns with your long-term goals and has the potential to generate positive outcomes.

Additionally, consider alternative financing options such as loans, grants, or partnerships to support your growth initiatives. Carefully assess the terms and conditions of any financing options and ensure that they align with your business's financial capabilities and objectives.

By effectively managing your business finances, you can make informed decisions, ensure profitability, and position your online venture for long-term success. Take the time to track your income and expenses, create a budget, manage your cash flow, set appropriate prices, and strategically invest in growth. With a solid financial foundation, you can navigate the challenges and opportunities of the online business landscape with confidence.

5.2 Budgeting and Cash Flow Management

———

One of the key aspects of running a successful online business is effectively managing your finances. Budgeting and cash flow management are essential skills that every online entrepreneur should master. By understanding and implementing sound financial practices, you can ensure the long-term sustainability and profitability of your business.

5.2.1 Importance of Budgeting

BUDGETING IS THE PROCESS of creating a financial plan for your business. It involves estimating your income and expenses over a specific period, typically on a monthly or yearly basis. Budgeting allows you to allocate your resources effectively, make informed financial decisions, and track your progress towards your financial goals.

Creating a budget for your online business provides several benefits. Firstly, it helps you gain a clear understanding of your financial situation. By analyzing your income and expenses, you can identify areas where you can cut costs or invest more resources. This knowledge enables you to make informed decisions about pricing, marketing strategies, and resource allocation.

Secondly, budgeting helps you prioritize your spending. By setting financial goals and allocating funds accordingly, you can ensure that your business's most critical needs are met. This includes investing in marketing, product development, customer service, and other areas that directly contribute to your business's growth and success.

Lastly, budgeting allows you to monitor your cash flow. Cash flow refers to the movement of money in and out of your business. By tracking your cash flow, you can identify potential cash shortages or surpluses and take proactive measures to address them. This ensures that you have enough liquidity to cover your expenses and seize growth opportunities when they arise.

5.2.2 Creating a Budget

TO CREATE AN EFFECTIVE budget for your online business, follow these steps:

1. **Estimate your income:** Start by estimating your expected revenue for the budget period. This includes sales from your products or services, affiliate marketing, advertising revenue, and any other sources of income. Be realistic and conservative in your estimates to avoid overestimating your revenue.
2. **Identify your fixed expenses:** Fixed expenses are recurring costs that remain relatively constant over time. These may include website hosting fees, software subscriptions, utilities, and other essential expenses. List down all your fixed expenses and their corresponding amounts.
3. **Account for variable expenses:** Variable expenses are

costs that fluctuate based on your business's activity level. This may include advertising expenses, inventory costs, shipping fees, and other variable costs. Estimate these expenses based on historical data or industry benchmarks.

4. **Consider one-time expenses:** One-time expenses are non-recurring costs that you anticipate during the budget period. This may include website redesign, equipment purchases, or hiring freelancers for specific projects. Identify these expenses and allocate funds accordingly.

5. **Factor in contingencies:** It's essential to set aside a portion of your budget for unexpected expenses or emergencies. This acts as a safety net and ensures that you have the flexibility to handle unforeseen circumstances without disrupting your business operations.

6. **Review and adjust:** Once you have estimated your income and expenses, review your budget to ensure that it aligns with your business goals and objectives. Make adjustments as necessary to optimize your resource allocation and ensure that your budget is realistic and achievable.

5.2.3 Cash Flow Management

CASH FLOW MANAGEMENT is the process of monitoring and optimizing the movement of money in and out of your business. It involves tracking your cash inflows and outflows, ensuring that you have enough cash on hand to cover your expenses, and maximizing the efficiency of your cash flow.

To effectively manage your cash flow, consider the following strategies:

1. **Monitor your cash flow:** Regularly review your cash flow statement to track the timing and amount of cash coming into and leaving your business. This will help you identify any cash flow gaps or surpluses and take appropriate action.

2. **Forecast your cash flow:** Use historical data and future projections to forecast your cash flow for the upcoming months or quarters. This will allow you to anticipate any potential cash shortages or surpluses and plan accordingly.

3. **Manage your receivables:** Implement effective invoicing and payment collection processes to ensure timely receipt of payments from your customers. Consider offering incentives for early payment or implementing a system to follow up on overdue invoices.

4. **Negotiate favorable payment terms:** When dealing with suppliers or service providers, negotiate payment terms that align with your cash flow needs. This may include extended payment terms, discounts for early payment, or installment options.

5. **Control your expenses:** Regularly review your expenses and identify areas where you can reduce costs without compromising the quality of your

products or services. This may involve renegotiating contracts, finding more cost-effective suppliers, or eliminating unnecessary expenses.

6. **Maintain a cash reserve:** Set aside a portion of your revenue as a cash reserve to cover unexpected expenses or cash flow gaps. This will provide you with a financial cushion and peace of mind during challenging times.

7. **Consider financing options:** If you anticipate a cash flow shortfall or need additional funds for growth opportunities, explore financing options such as business loans, lines of credit, or crowdfunding. However, carefully evaluate the terms and interest rates to ensure that it aligns with your business's financial goals.

By implementing these budgeting and cash flow management strategies, you can ensure the financial stability and success of your online business. Regularly review and update your budget, monitor your cash flow, and make informed financial decisions to drive growth and profitability. Remember, effective financial management is a continuous process that requires diligence and adaptability.

5.3 Pricing Strategies and Profitability

———

Pricing is a critical aspect of running a successful online business. It directly impacts your profitability and can determine the success or failure of your venture. In this section, we will explore various pricing strategies and discuss how to ensure profitability in your online business.

5.3.1 Understanding the Importance of Pricing

PRICING IS MORE THAN just assigning a value to your products or services. It is a strategic decision that requires careful consideration. The right pricing strategy can help you attract customers, differentiate yourself from competitors, and maximize your profits. On the other hand, poor pricing decisions can lead to financial losses and hinder your business growth.

When setting your prices, it is essential to consider factors such as production costs, market demand, competition, and perceived value. Understanding your target audience and their willingness to pay is crucial in determining the optimal price point for your offerings.

5.3.2 Cost-Based Pricing

COST-BASED PRICING is a straightforward approach where you calculate the cost of producing your product or delivering your service and add a markup to determine the selling price. This strategy ensures that you cover your costs and generate a profit. However, it does not take into account market demand or the perceived value of your offerings.

To implement cost-based pricing effectively, you need to accurately calculate your costs, including direct costs (materials, labor) and indirect costs (overhead, marketing expenses). It is also important to regularly review and update your pricing as your costs change over time.

5.3.3 Value-Based Pricing

VALUE-BASED PRICING focuses on the perceived value of your offerings to customers. Instead of solely relying on production costs, this strategy considers the benefits and outcomes that customers derive from your products or services. By aligning your prices with the value you provide, you can capture a fair share of the value you create for your customers.

To implement value-based pricing, you need to understand your target audience's needs, preferences, and the problems your offerings solve for them. Conduct market research, gather customer feedback, and analyze your competitors to determine the value your customers place on your offerings. This approach allows you to charge premium prices for high-value products or services.

5.3.4 Competitive Pricing

COMPETITIVE PRICING involves setting your prices based on what your competitors are charging for similar products or services. This strategy aims to position your offerings in line with the market and attract customers by offering comparable prices. However, it is important to consider your costs and profitability when adopting a competitive pricing strategy.

To implement competitive pricing, research your competitors' pricing strategies and analyze their value propositions. Determine whether you want to position yourself as a low-cost provider, a premium brand, or somewhere in between. It is crucial to regularly monitor your competitors' pricing and adjust your prices accordingly to stay competitive in the market.

5.3.5 Dynamic Pricing

DYNAMIC PRICING, ALSO known as demand-based pricing or surge pricing, involves adjusting your prices in real-time based on market demand, customer behavior, or other external factors. This strategy allows you to optimize your prices to maximize revenue and profitability.

Dynamic pricing is commonly used in industries such as travel, hospitality, and e-commerce, where demand fluctuates frequently. By leveraging data analytics and algorithms, you can set prices that reflect the current market conditions and customer preferences. However, it is important to strike a balance between maximizing revenue and maintaining customer trust and loyalty.

5.3.6 Bundling and Upselling

BUNDLING AND UPSELLING are effective pricing strategies that can increase your average transaction value and overall profitability. Bundling involves offering multiple products or services together at a discounted price, providing customers with added value and encouraging them to make a larger purchase.

Upselling, on the other hand, involves offering customers a higher-priced alternative or additional features to their initial purchase. By highlighting the benefits and value of the upsell, you can increase the customer's perceived value and generate additional revenue.

To implement bundling and upselling effectively, analyze your product or service offerings and identify complementary items or upgrades that can be bundled or upsold. Ensure that the bundled or upsold items provide significant value to the customer and are priced competitively.

5.3.7 Monitoring and Adjusting Prices

SETTING YOUR PRICES is not a one-time decision. It requires continuous monitoring and adjustment to ensure profitability and competitiveness. Regularly review your pricing strategy and analyze its impact on your business performance.

Monitor market trends, customer feedback, and changes in costs to identify opportunities for price adjustments. Consider conducting pricing experiments or A/B testing to gauge customer response to different price points. By collecting and analyzing data, you can make informed decisions about pricing changes that will optimize your profitability.

Remember that pricing is not solely about maximizing revenue. It is about finding the right balance between profitability, customer value, and market competitiveness. Continuously evaluate and refine your pricing strategy to ensure long-term success in your online business.

Conclusion

———

Pricing strategies play a crucial role in the profitability and success of your online business. By understanding the importance of pricing, considering different approaches such as cost-based, value-based, competitive, and dynamic pricing, and leveraging bundling and upselling techniques, you can optimize your prices to maximize profitability.

Regularly monitor and adjust your prices based on market conditions, customer feedback, and changes in costs. Remember that pricing is not a one-size-fits-all approach and requires continuous evaluation and refinement. By implementing effective pricing strategies, you can position your online business for long-term success and profitability.

5.4 Investing in Growth and Expansion

⸻

As an online entrepreneur, investing in growth and expansion is crucial for the long-term success of your business. In this section, we will explore the various strategies and considerations you need to keep in mind when it comes to investing in your online venture.

5.4.1 Assessing Growth Opportunities

BEFORE YOU CAN INVEST in growth and expansion, it's important to assess the various opportunities available to you. Start by analyzing your current business performance and identifying areas where you can potentially expand. This could include entering new markets, launching new products or services, or targeting a different customer segment.

Conduct market research to understand the demand for your offerings in different markets and evaluate the competition. Look for gaps in the market that you can fill with your unique value proposition. Additionally, consider the scalability of your business model and whether it can support growth without compromising quality or customer satisfaction.

5.4.2 Setting Growth Goals

ONCE YOU HAVE IDENTIFIED growth opportunities, it's essential to set clear and measurable goals. These goals will serve as a roadmap for your investment decisions and help you stay focused on your growth objectives. When setting growth goals, consider both short-term and long-term targets.

Short-term goals could include increasing website traffic, expanding your customer base, or launching a new product or service. Long-term goals may involve achieving a certain revenue milestone, expanding into international markets, or becoming a market leader in your industry.

Ensure that your goals are specific, measurable, attainable, relevant, and time-bound (SMART). This will help you track your progress and make informed decisions about your investments.

5.4.3 Financial Planning for Growth

INVESTING IN GROWTH and expansion requires careful financial planning. Start by assessing your current financial situation and determining how much capital you have available for investment. Consider whether you will need to seek external funding, such as loans or investments, to support your growth plans.

Create a detailed financial forecast that outlines your projected revenue, expenses, and cash flow for the period in which you plan to invest in growth. This will help you understand the financial implications of your investment decisions and ensure that you have sufficient resources to support your growth plans.

Additionally, consider the potential risks and uncertainties associated with your growth initiatives. Have contingency plans in place to mitigate any financial risks and ensure that you can adapt to unexpected challenges.

5.4.4 Strategic Partnerships and Collaborations

INVESTING IN GROWTH and expansion can be accelerated through strategic partnerships and collaborations. Look for opportunities to collaborate with other businesses or individuals who can complement your offerings or provide access to new markets.

Consider forming partnerships with suppliers, distributors, or complementary service providers. These partnerships can help you expand your reach, reduce costs, and leverage the expertise of others. Look for businesses that share similar values and have a track record of success.

When entering into partnerships, ensure that you have clear agreements in place that outline the roles, responsibilities, and expectations of each party. Regularly evaluate the performance of your partnerships and make adjustments as needed to ensure mutual success.

5.4.5 Technology and Infrastructure Investments

INVESTING IN TECHNOLOGY and infrastructure is often necessary to support the growth and expansion of your online business. Evaluate your current systems and processes to identify any gaps or inefficiencies that may hinder your growth.

Consider investing in tools and software that can automate repetitive tasks, streamline operations, and improve productivity. This could include customer relationship management (CRM) systems, project management tools, or e-commerce platforms.

Additionally, assess your website and online presence to ensure that it can handle increased traffic and transactions. Invest in website optimization, security measures, and scalability to provide a seamless experience for your customers as your business grows.

5.4.6 Continuous Learning and Skill Development

INVESTING IN YOUR OWN knowledge and skills is just as important as investing in your business. As an online entrepreneur, staying updated with industry trends and acquiring new skills is essential for driving growth and staying ahead of the competition.

Allocate time and resources for continuous learning and skill development. This could involve attending industry conferences, participating in online courses, or joining professional networks and communities. Surround yourself with like-minded individuals who can inspire and challenge you to reach new heights.

By investing in your own personal growth, you will be better equipped to make informed decisions, adapt to changing market dynamics, and lead your business to long-term success.

Conclusion

INVESTING IN GROWTH and expansion is a critical step in the journey of an online entrepreneur. By assessing growth opportunities, setting clear goals, and making strategic investments, you can position your business for long-term success. Remember to plan your finances carefully, explore strategic partnerships, invest in technology and infrastructure, and continuously invest in your own personal growth. With the right mindset and strategic approach, you can navigate the challenges and embrace the opportunities that come with growing your online venture.

Building an Online Community

6.1 Understanding the Importance of Community

———

In today's digital age, building an online community is crucial for the success of any online business. An online community refers to a group of individuals who share common interests, values, or goals and engage with each other through various online platforms. These communities can be a powerful tool for entrepreneurs to connect with their target audience, build brand loyalty, and drive business growth.

6.1.1 Connecting with Your Target Audience

ONE OF THE PRIMARY benefits of building an online community is the ability to connect with your target audience on a deeper level. By creating a space where like-minded individuals can come together, you can foster a sense of belonging and create a supportive environment for your customers or clients. This connection allows you to understand their needs, preferences, and pain points, enabling you to tailor your products or services to better meet their expectations.

6.1.2 Building Brand Loyalty

AN ONLINE COMMUNITY provides a platform for you to build brand loyalty among your customers. When individuals feel a sense of belonging to a community, they are more likely to develop a strong affinity for your brand. By actively engaging with your community members, addressing their concerns, and providing valuable content, you can establish trust and credibility, which in turn leads to increased customer loyalty. Loyal customers are not only more likely to make repeat purchases but also become advocates for your brand, spreading positive word-of-mouth and attracting new customers.

6.1.3 Driving Business Growth

A THRIVING ONLINE COMMUNITY can significantly contribute to the growth of your business. By fostering a sense of community, you create a space where customers can engage with each other and share their experiences. This user-generated content can serve as powerful social proof, influencing potential customers' purchasing decisions. Additionally, an active community can help generate valuable insights and feedback, allowing you to improve your products or services based on the needs and preferences of your customers. By leveraging the power of your community, you can drive organic growth and expand your customer base.

6.1.4 Enhancing Customer Support

AN ONLINE COMMUNITY can also serve as a valuable resource for customer support. By providing a platform where customers can ask questions, seek advice, and share their experiences, you can create a self-supporting ecosystem. Community members can help each other by sharing their knowledge and providing solutions to common problems. This not only reduces the burden on your customer support team but also creates a sense of empowerment among your customers, as they can rely on the community for assistance.

Prompt and effective customer support is essential for building a positive brand reputation and ensuring customer satisfaction.

6.1.5 Collaboration and Co-Creation

BUILDING AN ONLINE community opens up opportunities for collaboration and co-creation. By engaging with your community members, you can identify individuals who possess unique skills or expertise that can benefit your business. Collaborating with community members on projects, content creation, or product development can not only enhance the quality of your offerings but also foster a sense of ownership and pride among your community members. This collaborative approach can lead to innovative ideas, increased customer satisfaction, and ultimately, business growth.

6.1.6 Creating a Supportive Network

ENTREPRENEURSHIP CAN be a lonely journey, especially in the online space. Building an online community allows you to connect with fellow entrepreneurs, industry experts, and mentors who can provide guidance, support, and valuable insights. By actively participating in relevant communities, you can expand your network, learn from others' experiences, and stay updated with the latest industry trends. This supportive network can be a source of inspiration, motivation, and accountability, helping you overcome challenges and achieve your entrepreneurial goals.

6.1.7 Nurturing Long-Term Relationships

AN ONLINE COMMUNITY provides a platform for nurturing long-term relationships with your customers. By consistently engaging with your community members, providing valuable content, and addressing their needs, you can build trust and loyalty over time. These long-term relationships are essential for the sustainability and growth of your business. By focusing on building a community rather than just acquiring customers, you create a loyal customer base that is more likely to stay with you and continue to support your business in the long run.

In conclusion, building an online community is a vital aspect of online entrepreneurship. It allows you to connect with your target audience, build brand loyalty, drive business growth, enhance customer support, foster collaboration, and create a supportive network. By understanding the importance of community and actively investing in its development, you can unlock the full potential of your online venture and pave the way for long-term success.

6.2 Creating a Brand Community

I n today's digital age, building a strong brand community is essential for the success of any online business. A brand community is a group of loyal customers and followers who are passionate about your brand and actively engage with it. These communities not only provide a sense of belonging and connection for your customers but also serve as a powerful marketing tool for your business. By creating a brand community, you can foster customer loyalty, increase brand awareness, and drive customer engagement. In this section, we will explore the key strategies and tactics to create a thriving brand community for your online business.

6.2.1 Understanding the Importance of Brand Community

A BRAND COMMUNITY GOES beyond just having a group of customers who purchase your products or services. It is about creating a sense of belonging and building a relationship with your customers. When customers feel connected to your brand and have a community to engage with, they are more likely to become loyal advocates who not only continue to support your business but also spread the word to others.

A brand community can provide several benefits for your online business, including:

1. **Customer Loyalty:** By fostering a sense of community, you can cultivate strong relationships with your customers, leading to increased loyalty and repeat purchases.

2. **Word-of-Mouth Marketing:** A brand community can become a powerful marketing tool as satisfied customers share their positive experiences with others, leading to organic growth and new customer acquisition.

3. **Feedback and Insights:** Engaging with your brand community allows you to gather valuable feedback and insights directly from your customers. This feedback can help you improve your products, services, and overall customer experience.

4. **Co-Creation and Innovation:** A brand community can be a source of inspiration and ideas for new products or services. By involving your community in the co-creation process, you can tap into their creativity and innovation.

5. **Brand Advocacy:** When customers feel a strong connection to your brand, they are more likely to become brand advocates who actively promote your business to their networks, further expanding your reach and influence.

6.2.2 Building a Brand Community

BUILDING A BRAND COMMUNITY requires a strategic approach and consistent effort. Here are some key steps to help you create a thriving brand community for your online business:

Identify Your Target Audience

TO BUILD A BRAND COMMUNITY, it is crucial to identify and understand your target audience. Who are your ideal customers? What are their interests, needs, and pain points? By gaining a deep understanding of your target audience, you can tailor your community-building efforts to resonate with them and provide value.

Define Your Brand Values and Purpose

YOUR BRAND VALUES AND purpose are the foundation of your brand community. Clearly define what your brand stands for and the purpose it serves. This will attract like-minded individuals who align with your values and are more likely to engage with your community.

Choose the Right Platform

SELECTING THE RIGHT platform to host your brand community is essential. Consider the preferences and behaviors of your target audience. Are they more active on social media platforms like Facebook or Instagram? Or do they prefer dedicated community platforms like Slack or Discord? Choose a platform that aligns with your audience's preferences and provides the necessary features for community engagement.

Create Engaging Content

CONTENT IS THE FUEL that drives engagement within your brand community. Create and share valuable, relevant, and engaging content that resonates with your audience. This can include blog posts, videos, podcasts, or even live events. Encourage community members to contribute their own content and foster a culture of collaboration and knowledge sharing.

Foster Two-Way Communication

BUILDING A BRAND COMMUNITY is not just about broadcasting your message; it's about fostering meaningful conversations and interactions. Encourage two-way communication by actively listening to your community members, responding to their comments and questions, and seeking their input and feedback. This will make them feel valued and appreciated, strengthening their connection to your brand.

Organize Events and Activities

ORGANIZING EVENTS AND activities can help foster a sense of community and bring your members together. This can include virtual meetups, webinars, workshops, or even physical gatherings if feasible. These events provide opportunities for community members to connect, learn from each other, and deepen their engagement with your brand.

Recognize and Reward Community Members

RECOGNIZING AND REWARDING your community members is crucial for building loyalty and encouraging active participation. Highlight and celebrate the achievements and contributions of your community members. This can be done through shoutouts, exclusive perks, or even gamification elements like badges or levels. By acknowledging their efforts, you create a positive and supportive environment that encourages continued engagement.

6.2.3 Measuring and Improving Community Engagement

MEASURING THE SUCCESS of your brand community is essential to understand its impact and identify areas for improvement. Here are some key metrics to consider when evaluating community engagement:

1. **Membership Growth:** Track the number of new members joining your community over time. This metric indicates the growth and reach of your brand community.
2. **Active Participation:** Measure the level of engagement within your community by tracking the number of active members, comments, likes, and shares. This metric reflects the level of interest and involvement of your community members.
3. **Retention Rate:** Monitor the percentage of community members who continue to engage with your brand over time. A high retention rate indicates

a strong and loyal community.

4. **Referral Rate:** Measure the number of new community members acquired through referrals from existing members. A high referral rate indicates a satisfied and engaged community.

5. **Feedback and Sentiment:** Regularly collect feedback from your community members to gauge their satisfaction and sentiment towards your brand. This can be done through surveys, polls, or direct conversations.

Based on the insights gathered from these metrics, you can make data-driven decisions to improve community engagement. Experiment with different strategies, content formats, and activities to keep your community members engaged and excited about being part of your brand community.

Conclusion

CREATING A BRAND COMMUNITY is a powerful way to foster customer loyalty, increase brand awareness, and drive customer engagement. By following the strategies outlined in this section, you can build a thriving brand community for your online business. Remember, building a brand community takes time and consistent effort, but the rewards are well worth it. Invest in your community, listen to your members, and provide value, and you will create a community that not only supports your business but also becomes a driving force behind its success.

6.3 Engaging and Retaining Community Members

Building an online community is not just about attracting members; it's also about engaging and retaining them. A thriving community is one where members feel valued, connected, and motivated to actively participate. In this section, we will explore strategies and best practices for engaging and retaining community members, ensuring the long-term success of your online community.

6.3.1 Understanding the Importance of Engagement

ENGAGEMENT IS THE LIFEBLOOD of any online community. It is the measure of how involved and active your community members are. Engaged members are more likely to contribute, share ideas, and participate in discussions, which ultimately leads to a vibrant and dynamic community. Here are some reasons why engagement is crucial:

1. **Fosters a sense of belonging:** When community members feel connected to each other and the community as a whole, they are more likely to stay engaged and invested in its growth.
2. **Encourages collaboration:** Engaged members are more willing to collaborate, share knowledge, and help each other, creating a supportive and

collaborative environment.

3. **Drives innovation:** Active engagement leads to the exchange of ideas and perspectives, fostering innovation and creativity within the community.

4. **Increases loyalty:** Engaged members are more likely to become loyal advocates for your brand or community, promoting it to others and attracting new members.

6.3.2 Strategies for Engaging Community Members

NOW THAT WE UNDERSTAND the importance of engagement, let's explore some strategies to effectively engage your community members:

1. **Create valuable content:** Regularly share high-quality content that is relevant and valuable to your community. This can include blog posts, articles, videos, podcasts, or any other form of content that educates, entertains, or inspires your members.

2. **Encourage active participation:** Actively encourage your community members to participate by asking questions, starting discussions, and seeking their opinions. Make them feel heard and valued by responding to their contributions and acknowledging their input.

3. **Organize events and challenges:** Plan and host events, challenges, or contests that encourage members to actively engage with each other and the community. This could be a webinar, a virtual conference, a monthly challenge, or a collaborative

project.

4. **Facilitate networking opportunities:** Provide platforms or spaces for community members to connect and network with each other. This can be through online forums, social media groups, or even virtual meetups. Encourage members to share their experiences, collaborate on projects, and build relationships.

5. **Recognize and reward contributions:** Acknowledge and appreciate the contributions of your community members. This can be done through shoutouts, featuring their work or achievements, or even offering exclusive perks or rewards for active participation.

6. **Provide valuable resources:** Offer resources, tools, or exclusive content that is only accessible to community members. This creates a sense of exclusivity and incentivizes members to stay engaged.

7. **Be responsive and accessible:** Be responsive to member inquiries, feedback, and suggestions. Make yourself accessible through various channels such as email, social media, or a dedicated community platform. Show that you value their input and are committed to their success.

6.3.3 Retaining Community Members

ENGAGING COMMUNITY members is essential, but equally important is retaining them. Retention ensures the long-term sustainability and growth of your community. Here are some strategies to help you retain community members:

1. **Build relationships:** Foster genuine connections with your community members. Take the time to get to know them, understand their needs, and build relationships based on trust and mutual respect. This creates a sense of loyalty and belonging.

2. **Provide ongoing value:** Continuously provide value to your community members by sharing valuable content, resources, and insights. Keep them informed about industry trends, best practices, and new opportunities. Be the go-to resource for their needs.

3. **Offer exclusive benefits:** Provide exclusive benefits or perks to your community members. This could include discounts on products or services, early access to new features or content, or access to premium resources. Make them feel special and appreciated.

4. **Encourage collaboration:** Facilitate collaboration among community members by creating opportunities for them to work together on projects, share expertise, or collaborate on initiatives. This fosters a sense of camaraderie and strengthens the bonds within the community.

5. **Continuously improve:** Regularly seek feedback from your community members and use it to improve your community. Ask for suggestions, conduct surveys, or host feedback sessions to understand their needs and expectations. Actively implement changes based on their feedback.

6. **Celebrate milestones:** Recognize and celebrate the achievements and milestones of your community members. This can be done through public

acknowledgments, awards, or even hosting virtual celebrations. Make them feel valued and appreciated for their contributions.

Remember, building and retaining an engaged community takes time and effort. It requires consistent communication, valuable content, and a genuine commitment to the success and well-being of your community members. By implementing these strategies, you can create a thriving online community that fosters collaboration, innovation, and long-term success.

6.4 Leveraging User-Generated Content

―――

In today's digital age, user-generated content (UGC) has become a powerful tool for online entrepreneurs to engage with their audience, build trust, and drive growth. User-generated content refers to any form of content, such as reviews, testimonials, photos, videos, or social media posts, that is created by your customers or audience members. Leveraging UGC can have a significant impact on your online business, as it not only helps in building a sense of community but also serves as social proof and authenticates your brand.

6.4.1 The Power of User-Generated Content

USER-GENERATED CONTENT holds immense power in the online world. It allows your customers to become advocates for your brand and share their experiences with others. Here are some key benefits of leveraging user-generated content:

Building Trust and Authenticity

WHEN POTENTIAL CUSTOMERS see real people sharing their positive experiences with your brand, it builds trust and authenticity. User-generated content acts as social proof, showing that your products or services are genuinely valuable and reliable. It helps to overcome skepticism and encourages others to engage with your brand.

Increasing Engagement and Reach

USER-GENERATED CONTENT has the potential to go viral and reach a wider audience. When your customers create and share content related to your brand, it increases engagement and encourages others to join the conversation. This can lead to increased brand awareness and exposure, ultimately driving more traffic to your website or social media platforms.

Enhancing SEO and Search Rankings

USER-GENERATED CONTENT can also have a positive impact on your search engine optimization (SEO) efforts. When customers create content that includes relevant keywords and links to your website, it can improve your search rankings. Additionally, UGC often includes natural language and long-tail keywords, which can help your website rank for specific search queries.

Fostering a Sense of Community

BY ENCOURAGING YOUR audience to create and share content, you can foster a sense of community around your brand. This creates a space for your customers to connect with each other, share their experiences, and provide support. A strong brand community can lead to increased loyalty and advocacy, as customers feel a sense of belonging and connection.

6.4.2 Strategies for Leveraging User-Generated Content

TO EFFECTIVELY LEVERAGE user-generated content, you need to implement strategies that encourage your audience to create and share content related to your brand. Here are some strategies to consider:

Encourage Reviews and Testimonials

ONE OF THE MOST COMMON forms of user-generated content is reviews and testimonials. Encourage your customers to leave reviews on your website or third-party review platforms. Offer incentives, such as discounts or exclusive content, to motivate them to share their experiences. Display these reviews prominently on your website to build trust and credibility.

Run Contests and Giveaways

CONTESTS AND GIVEAWAYS are a great way to encourage your audience to create and share content. Ask them to submit photos, videos, or stories related to your brand, and offer prizes for the best submissions. This not only generates user-generated content but also creates excitement and engagement around your brand.

Create Branded Hashtags

BRANDED HASHTAGS CAN help you track and collect user-generated content on social media platforms. Encourage your audience to use these hashtags when sharing content related to your brand. This allows you to easily find and repost their content, increasing its visibility and reach.

Feature User-Generated Content

SHOWCASING USER-GENERATED content on your website and social media platforms is a powerful way to engage with your audience and encourage others to create content. Feature customer photos, videos, or testimonials on your website's homepage or product pages. Share user-generated content on your social media accounts and give credit to the creators. This not only acknowledges and appreciates your customers but also motivates others to contribute.

Engage and Interact with User-Generated Content

WHEN YOUR AUDIENCE creates and shares content related to your brand, make sure to engage and interact with them. Like, comment, and share their content to show appreciation. Respond to their comments and messages to build a personal connection. By actively engaging with user-generated content, you encourage more participation and strengthen the bond between your brand and your audience.

6.4.3 Best Practices for User-Generated Content

WHILE LEVERAGING USER-generated content can be highly beneficial, it's essential to follow some best practices to ensure a positive and authentic experience for both your brand and your audience. Here are some best practices to consider:

Obtain Consent and Rights

BEFORE USING ANY USER-generated content, always obtain consent from the creator and ensure that you have the necessary rights to use and share the content. This helps protect both your brand and the content creator from any legal issues.

Monitor and Moderate

MONITOR AND MODERATE user-generated content to ensure that it aligns with your brand values and guidelines. Remove any content that is inappropriate, offensive, or violates your terms of service. By maintaining a positive and safe environment, you can encourage more meaningful and valuable user-generated content.

Give Credit and Recognition

ALWAYS GIVE CREDIT and recognition to the creators of user-generated content. Tag them, mention their usernames, or include their names in the captions. This not only shows appreciation but also encourages others to contribute.

Be Transparent and Authentic

WHEN LEVERAGING USER-generated content, be transparent and authentic. Clearly disclose if any incentives were provided for creating the content. Avoid manipulating or misrepresenting user-generated content to maintain trust and credibility.

Engage and Respond

AS MENTIONED EARLIER, actively engage and respond to user-generated content. Show appreciation, answer questions, and address any concerns. By actively participating in the conversation, you foster a sense of community and build stronger relationships with your audience.

Conclusion

LEVERAGING USER-GENERATED content can be a game-changer for your online business. By encouraging your audience to create and share content related to your brand, you can build trust, increase engagement, and foster a sense of community. Implement the strategies and best practices discussed in this section to effectively leverage user-generated content and unlock its full potential for your online venture.

Scaling Your Online Business

7.1 Identifying Growth Opportunities

———

A s an online entrepreneur, one of your primary goals is to grow your business and expand your reach. Identifying growth opportunities is crucial for taking your online venture to the next level. In this section, we will explore various strategies and techniques to help you identify and capitalize on growth opportunities.

7.1.1 Analyzing Market Trends

TO IDENTIFY GROWTH opportunities, it is essential to stay informed about the latest market trends and industry developments. Conducting thorough market research will provide you with valuable insights into consumer behavior, emerging technologies, and competitive landscapes. By analyzing market trends, you can identify gaps in the market, spot emerging niches, and adapt your business strategies accordingly.

Start by monitoring industry publications, attending conferences and webinars, and following influential thought leaders in your field. Stay updated with the latest news and developments in your industry to identify potential growth opportunities before your competitors do. By understanding the evolving needs and preferences of your target audience, you can position your business to meet those demands effectively.

7.1.2 Leveraging Data Analytics

DATA ANALYTICS PLAYS a crucial role in identifying growth opportunities for your online business. By leveraging data, you can gain valuable insights into customer behavior, preferences, and purchasing patterns. Analyzing data can help you identify areas of improvement, optimize your marketing strategies, and make data-driven decisions to drive growth.

Start by implementing robust analytics tools such as Google Analytics or other similar platforms to track and measure key performance indicators (KPIs) relevant to your business. Analyze website traffic, conversion rates, customer demographics, and engagement metrics to gain a comprehensive understanding of your audience and their preferences. Use this data to identify areas where you can improve customer experience, optimize your marketing campaigns, and identify new opportunities for growth.

7.1.3 Expanding Your Product or Service Offering

EXPANDING YOUR PRODUCT or service offering is an effective way to drive growth in your online business. By diversifying your offerings, you can attract new customers, increase customer loyalty, and tap into new market segments. Consider conducting market research to identify potential product or service extensions that align with your target audience's needs and preferences.

Start by analyzing your existing customer base and identifying any common pain points or unmet needs. Use this information to develop new products or services that address these gaps. Additionally, consider cross-selling or upselling opportunities to your existing customer base. By offering complementary products or services, you can increase customer satisfaction and generate additional revenue streams.

7.1.4 Exploring New Marketing Channels

EXPLORING NEW MARKETING channels can help you reach a wider audience and drive growth for your online business. While you may already have established marketing channels, such as social media or email marketing, it is essential to stay open to new opportunities and experiment with different platforms.

Research emerging marketing channels and platforms that align with your target audience's preferences. For example, if your target audience consists of younger demographics, consider leveraging platforms like TikTok or Snapchat to reach them effectively. By diversifying your marketing channels, you can expand your reach and attract new customers who may not be present on your existing platforms.

7.1.5 Collaborating with Strategic Partners

COLLABORATING WITH strategic partners can open up new growth opportunities for your online business. Strategic partnerships allow you to leverage the expertise, resources, and customer base of other businesses to drive mutual growth. Look for businesses or individuals in complementary industries or with a similar target audience to explore potential collaboration opportunities.

Consider partnerships such as joint marketing campaigns, co-creating content, or cross-promotions. By collaborating with strategic partners, you can tap into their existing customer base, gain exposure to new audiences, and benefit from shared resources and expertise. Strategic partnerships can be a powerful growth strategy, enabling you to expand your reach and drive mutual success.

7.1.6 Listening to Customer Feedback

LISTENING TO CUSTOMER feedback is crucial for identifying growth opportunities and improving your online business. Your customers are a valuable source of insights and can provide you with valuable feedback on your products, services, and overall customer experience. Actively seek feedback from your customers through surveys, reviews, and social media interactions.

Analyze customer feedback to identify areas where you can improve and innovate. Look for common themes or suggestions that can help you enhance your offerings or address pain points. By listening to your customers and incorporating their feedback into your business strategies, you can build stronger customer relationships, improve customer satisfaction, and drive growth.

7.1.7 Monitoring Competitors

MONITORING YOUR COMPETITORS is essential for identifying growth opportunities and staying ahead in the online business landscape. Keep a close eye on your competitors' strategies, offerings, and marketing campaigns. Analyze their strengths and weaknesses to identify areas where you can differentiate yourself and capitalize on untapped market segments.

By monitoring your competitors, you can identify gaps in the market that they may have overlooked or areas where you can offer a superior product or service. Additionally, studying your competitors can provide you with valuable insights into emerging trends and customer preferences. Use this information to refine your own strategies and position your business for growth.

Identifying growth opportunities is an ongoing process that requires continuous monitoring, analysis, and adaptation. By staying informed, leveraging data, expanding your offerings, exploring new marketing channels, collaborating with strategic partners, listening to customer feedback, and monitoring your competitors, you can identify and capitalize on growth opportunities to take your online business to new heights.

7.2 Developing Scalable Systems and Processes

As your online business grows, it becomes crucial to develop scalable systems and processes that can handle increased demand and ensure smooth operations. Scaling your business requires careful planning and implementation of efficient systems that can accommodate growth without sacrificing quality or customer satisfaction. In this section, we will explore the key steps to developing scalable systems and processes for your online business.

7.2.1 Assessing Current Systems and Processes

BEFORE YOU CAN DEVELOP scalable systems and processes, it is essential to assess your current operations. Take a close look at your existing systems and processes to identify any bottlenecks or areas that may hinder scalability. This assessment will help you understand the strengths and weaknesses of your current operations and provide a foundation for improvement.

Start by mapping out your existing processes and workflows. Identify any manual or repetitive tasks that can be automated to save time and resources. Look for areas where you can streamline operations and eliminate unnecessary steps. By understanding your current systems and processes, you can identify areas for improvement and develop a roadmap for scalability.

7.2.2 Streamlining and Automating Processes

ONE OF THE KEY ASPECTS of developing scalable systems and processes is streamlining and automating tasks wherever possible. Automation can help reduce human error, increase efficiency, and free up valuable time for you and your team to focus on more strategic activities.

Start by identifying tasks that can be automated using technology or software solutions. This could include automating email marketing campaigns, order processing, inventory management, or customer support. Look for tools and platforms that can integrate with your existing systems and automate repetitive tasks.

Additionally, consider implementing standardized processes and workflows to ensure consistency and efficiency across your operations. Documenting these processes will not only help streamline your current operations but also make it easier to train new employees as your business grows.

7.2.3 Implementing Scalable Technology Infrastructure

TO SUPPORT THE SCALABILITY of your online business, it is crucial to have a robust and scalable technology infrastructure in place. This includes your website, hosting provider, e-commerce platform, and any other software or tools you rely on to run your business.

Ensure that your website and hosting provider can handle increased traffic and transactions as your business grows. Consider using a content delivery network (CDN) to improve website performance and load times. Evaluate your e-commerce platform to ensure it can handle a higher volume of orders and integrate with other systems seamlessly.

Investing in cloud-based solutions can also provide scalability and flexibility. Cloud computing allows you to scale your infrastructure up or down based on demand, ensuring that you only pay for the resources you need. This can be particularly beneficial during peak seasons or promotional periods when your website experiences a surge in traffic.

7.2.4 Building a Scalable Team

AS YOUR ONLINE BUSINESS scales, it is essential to build a team that can support your growth. Hiring and training the right people is crucial to developing scalable systems and processes. Look for individuals who are adaptable, have a growth mindset, and can handle increased responsibilities as your business expands.

Consider outsourcing certain tasks or hiring freelancers to handle specific functions. This can provide flexibility and scalability without the need for full-time employees. Outsourcing can be particularly beneficial for non-core activities such as graphic design, content creation, or customer support.

Invest in training and development programs to upskill your team and ensure they have the necessary knowledge and skills to support your growing business. Encourage a culture of continuous learning and improvement to foster innovation and adaptability within your team.

7.2.5 Monitoring and Iterating

DEVELOPING SCALABLE systems and processes is an ongoing process. It is essential to continuously monitor and evaluate the effectiveness of your systems and make necessary adjustments as your business evolves.

Regularly review key performance indicators (KPIs) to assess the performance of your systems and processes. Look for areas where you can further optimize efficiency or improve customer experience. Solicit feedback from your team and customers to gain insights into areas that may require improvement.

Iterate and refine your systems and processes based on the feedback and data you collect. Embrace a culture of continuous improvement and adaptability to ensure that your systems can scale with your business.

Conclusion

DEVELOPING SCALABLE systems and processes is a critical step in scaling your online business. By assessing your current operations, streamlining and automating processes, implementing a scalable technology infrastructure, building a scalable team, and continuously monitoring and iterating, you can create a solid foundation for growth and success. Remember that scalability requires careful planning and a commitment to ongoing improvement. Embrace the challenge and seize the opportunities that come with scaling your online business.

7.3 Outsourcing and Delegating

―――

As your online business grows, it becomes increasingly important to leverage your time and resources effectively. One of the key strategies for scaling your business is outsourcing and delegating tasks to others. By doing so, you can focus on high-value activities that drive growth and profitability, while leaving routine and time-consuming tasks to capable professionals. In this section, we will explore the benefits of outsourcing and delegating, how to identify tasks to outsource, and best practices for managing outsourced work.

7.3.1 The Benefits of Outsourcing and Delegating

OUTSOURCING AND DELEGATING tasks can bring numerous benefits to your online business. Here are some of the key advantages:

1. **Time and Resource Optimization**: By outsourcing routine tasks, you free up your time to focus on strategic activities that require your expertise. This allows you to make better use of your time and resources, ultimately leading to increased productivity and efficiency.

2. **Access to Expertise**: Outsourcing allows you to tap into the expertise of professionals who specialize in specific areas. Whether it's web design, content creation, or customer support, outsourcing enables

you to work with skilled individuals who can deliver high-quality results.

3. **Cost Savings**: Outsourcing can be a cost-effective solution for your business. Instead of hiring full-time employees, you can engage freelancers or agencies on a project basis, saving on overhead costs such as salaries, benefits, and office space.

4. **Flexibility and Scalability**: Outsourcing provides the flexibility to scale your business up or down as needed. You can easily adjust the amount of work you outsource based on your business requirements, allowing you to adapt to changing market conditions quickly.

5. **Increased Focus on Core Competencies**: By delegating non-core tasks, you can concentrate on activities that align with your core competencies and business goals. This enables you to deliver exceptional value to your customers and differentiate yourself from competitors.

7.3.2 Identifying Tasks to Outsource

TO DETERMINE WHICH tasks to outsource, it's essential to evaluate your strengths, weaknesses, and the specific needs of your business. Here are some key considerations:

1. **Non-Core Activities**: Identify tasks that are necessary for your business but do not directly contribute to your core operations. These tasks can include administrative work, bookkeeping, graphic design, or social media management.

2. **Time-Consuming Tasks**: Look for tasks that consume a significant amount of your time but can be handled by others. This could include data entry, customer support, or content creation.

3. **Specialized Skills**: Consider tasks that require specialized skills or knowledge that you may not possess. Examples include web development, search engine optimization (SEO), or digital advertising.

4. **Repetitive Tasks**: Identify tasks that are repetitive in nature and can be easily documented and handed off to others. This could include email management, data analysis, or inventory management.

5. **Seasonal or Project-Based Work**: If your business experiences seasonal fluctuations or requires specific projects to be completed, outsourcing can provide the flexibility to handle these temporary demands without the need for long-term commitments.

7.3.3 Best Practices for Managing Outsourced Work

ONCE YOU HAVE IDENTIFIED the tasks to outsource, it's crucial to manage the outsourced work effectively to ensure successful outcomes. Here are some best practices to consider:

1. **Clearly Define Expectations**: Clearly communicate your expectations, deadlines, and deliverables to the outsourced professionals. Provide detailed instructions and guidelines to ensure they understand your requirements.

2. **Establish Effective Communication Channels**: Set

up regular communication channels to stay in touch with the outsourced team. This could include weekly meetings, email updates, or project management tools. Clear and timely communication is essential for successful collaboration.

3. **Monitor Progress and Quality**: Regularly review the progress of the outsourced work and assess the quality of the deliverables. Provide constructive feedback and address any issues promptly to ensure that the work meets your standards.

4. **Build Relationships**: Treat your outsourced professionals as valuable members of your team. Foster a positive working relationship by showing appreciation for their efforts, providing feedback, and offering opportunities for growth and development.

5. **Protect Intellectual Property**: If you are outsourcing tasks that involve sensitive information or intellectual property, ensure that appropriate confidentiality agreements are in place to protect your business interests.

6. **Evaluate Performance**: Periodically evaluate the performance of your outsourced professionals. Assess their ability to meet deadlines, deliver quality work, and align with your business objectives. If necessary, make adjustments or consider alternative outsourcing options.

7. **Continuously Improve Processes**: As you gain experience with outsourcing, look for ways to improve your processes and make them more efficient. Learn from past experiences and refine your

outsourcing strategy to maximize its benefits.

By effectively outsourcing and delegating tasks, you can streamline your operations, focus on strategic activities, and scale your online business more efficiently. Embrace the power of outsourcing and leverage the expertise of professionals to propel your business towards greater success.

Remember, outsourcing is not a one-size-fits-all solution. Evaluate your business needs, consider the advantages and challenges, and make informed decisions about which tasks to outsource. With careful planning and effective management, outsourcing can become a valuable tool in your entrepreneurial journey.

7.4 Managing Growth Challenges

———

As your online business begins to grow and expand, you will inevitably face a new set of challenges. Managing growth can be both exciting and overwhelming, but with the right strategies and mindset, you can navigate these challenges successfully. In this section, we will explore some common growth challenges that online entrepreneurs face and discuss effective ways to manage them.

7.4.1 Scaling Infrastructure and Resources

ONE OF THE FIRST CHALLENGES you may encounter when scaling your online business is the need to upgrade your infrastructure and allocate resources effectively. As your customer base grows, you may experience increased website traffic, higher demand for your products or services, and a greater need for customer support. It is crucial to assess your current infrastructure and determine if it can handle the increased workload.

Investing in scalable systems and processes is essential to ensure smooth operations as your business expands. Consider upgrading your website hosting plan to accommodate higher traffic, implementing customer relationship management (CRM) software to streamline customer support, and automating repetitive tasks to free up time for strategic initiatives.

Additionally, you may need to hire additional staff or outsource certain tasks to meet the growing demands of your business. Evaluate your current team's capabilities and identify areas where additional expertise or manpower is required. Outsourcing certain functions, such as accounting or content creation, can help you focus on core business activities while ensuring efficiency and quality.

7.4.2 Maintaining Quality and Consistency

AS YOUR BUSINESS GROWS, maintaining the same level of quality and consistency can become a challenge. It is essential to ensure that your products or services continue to meet customer expectations, even as you scale. Inconsistent quality can damage your reputation and lead to customer dissatisfaction.

To maintain quality and consistency, establish clear processes and standards for your operations. Document your workflows, train your team members, and regularly review and improve your processes. Implement quality control measures to ensure that every product or service meets your defined standards.

Regularly gathering customer feedback and monitoring customer satisfaction can also help you identify areas for improvement. Use customer feedback to make necessary adjustments and continuously enhance your offerings. Remember, delivering a consistent and exceptional customer experience is crucial for long-term success.

7.4.3 Managing Cash Flow

MANAGING CASH FLOW becomes increasingly important as your business grows. Rapid growth can strain your financial resources, and it is crucial to have a solid understanding of your cash flow to ensure sustainability and avoid cash flow gaps.

Develop a comprehensive financial plan that includes forecasting your revenue and expenses. Regularly monitor your cash flow and identify potential bottlenecks or areas where you may need additional funding. Consider working with a financial advisor or accountant to help you manage your finances effectively.

Implementing efficient invoicing and payment systems can also help improve cash flow. Offer multiple payment options to your customers and consider implementing automated payment reminders to reduce late payments. Negotiate favorable payment terms with suppliers to optimize your cash flow.

7.4.4 Adapting to Changing Market Dynamics

THE ONLINE BUSINESS landscape is dynamic, and market trends can change rapidly. As your business grows, it is essential to stay updated with industry trends and adapt your strategies accordingly. Failing to adapt to changing market dynamics can result in missed opportunities and loss of competitive advantage.

Stay informed about industry news, emerging technologies, and consumer behavior. Engage in continuous learning and professional development to enhance your knowledge and skills. Attend industry conferences, join relevant online communities, and network with other entrepreneurs to stay connected and gain valuable insights.

Regularly review and analyze your business performance and market trends. Identify areas where you can innovate and differentiate yourself from competitors. Be open to experimenting with new strategies and approaches to stay ahead of the curve.

7.4.5 Balancing Growth and Customer Experience

AS YOUR BUSINESS GROWS, it is crucial to strike a balance between scaling your operations and maintaining a positive customer experience. Rapid growth can sometimes lead to a decline in customer service quality if not managed effectively.

Invest in customer relationship management (CRM) systems to ensure personalized and efficient customer interactions. Train your customer support team to handle increased volumes without compromising on quality. Implement self-service options, such as FAQs or chatbots, to provide quick and convenient support to your customers.

Regularly gather customer feedback and use it to improve your processes and offerings. Continuously monitor customer satisfaction metrics and address any issues promptly.

Remember, happy and satisfied customers are more likely to become loyal advocates for your brand.

7.4.6 Building a Scalable Team

AS YOUR BUSINESS GROWS, building a scalable team becomes crucial to support your expansion. Hiring the right people and creating a strong organizational structure is essential for long-term success.

Define clear roles and responsibilities for each team member and ensure that they align with your business objectives. Hire individuals who are not only skilled but also share your vision and values. Foster a positive and collaborative work culture that encourages innovation and growth.

Consider implementing training and development programs to enhance the skills of your team members. Encourage continuous learning and provide opportunities for career advancement within your organization. Regularly assess your team's performance and provide constructive feedback to help them grow and excel.

7.4.7 Managing Risks and Uncertainties

AS YOUR BUSINESS GROWS, it is important to be prepared for potential risks and uncertainties. Rapid growth can expose your business to new challenges and vulnerabilities.

Identify potential risks and develop contingency plans to mitigate them. Regularly review and update your business continuity plan to ensure that you are prepared for unforeseen events. Consider investing in insurance coverage to protect your business against potential liabilities.

Stay informed about legal and regulatory requirements that may impact your business. Consult with legal and financial professionals to ensure compliance and minimize legal risks.

Maintain open lines of communication with your team and stakeholders. Encourage transparency and create a culture where everyone feels comfortable reporting potential risks or issues. Regularly review and assess your risk management strategies to ensure their effectiveness.

Managing growth challenges requires a proactive and strategic approach. By anticipating potential obstacles and implementing effective strategies, you can navigate the complexities of scaling your online business successfully. Embrace growth as an opportunity for learning and improvement, and remember to celebrate your achievements along the way.

Customer Relationship Management

8.1 Understanding Customer Relationship Management

———

Customer Relationship Management (CRM) is a vital aspect of running a successful online business. It involves managing and nurturing relationships with your customers to enhance their satisfaction, loyalty, and overall experience with your brand. In today's competitive digital landscape, building strong customer relationships is crucial for long-term success and sustainable growth.

8.1.1 The Importance of Customer Relationship Management

EFFECTIVE CRM IS ESSENTIAL for several reasons. Firstly, it helps you understand your customers better. By collecting and analyzing data about their preferences, behaviors, and needs, you can gain valuable insights that enable you to tailor your products, services, and marketing strategies to meet their expectations.

Secondly, CRM allows you to build customer loyalty. When you establish a strong connection with your customers and consistently deliver exceptional experiences, they are more likely to remain loyal to your brand, make repeat purchases, and even become advocates who refer others to your business.

Furthermore, CRM helps you identify and address customer issues promptly. By actively listening to your customers and providing timely support, you can resolve any problems they may encounter, ensuring their satisfaction and preventing negative word-of-mouth.

Lastly, effective CRM enables you to maximize customer lifetime value. By nurturing relationships with your existing customers, you can encourage repeat purchases, upsells, and cross-sells, ultimately increasing their overall value to your business.

8.1.2 Implementing Customer Relationship Management Strategies

TO IMPLEMENT EFFECTIVE CRM strategies, consider the following key steps:

8.1.2.1 Collecting Customer Data

START BY COLLECTING relevant data about your customers. This can include demographic information, purchase history, website interactions, and feedback. Utilize various tools and technologies, such as customer relationship management software, analytics platforms, and surveys, to gather this data.

8.1.2.2 Segmenting Your Customer Base

ONCE YOU HAVE COLLECTED customer data, segment your customer base into distinct groups based on common characteristics or behaviors. This segmentation allows you to tailor your marketing messages and offers to each group's specific needs and preferences.

8.1.2.3 Personalizing Customer Interactions

PERSONALIZATION IS key to effective CRM. Use the data you have collected to personalize your interactions with customers. Address them by their names, recommend products or services based on their previous purchases, and send personalized emails or offers. This level of personalization shows your customers that you value their individual needs and preferences.

8.1.2.4 Providing Exceptional Customer Service

EXCEPTIONAL CUSTOMER service is a cornerstone of CRM. Respond promptly to customer inquiries and provide support through various channels, such as email, live chat, or social media. Train your customer service team to be knowledgeable, empathetic, and proactive in resolving customer issues.

8.1.2.5 Building Customer Loyalty Programs

IMPLEMENT CUSTOMER loyalty programs to reward and incentivize repeat purchases. Offer exclusive discounts, early access to new products, or special perks to your loyal customers. These programs not only encourage customer retention but also foster a sense of belonging and appreciation.

8.1.2.6 Engaging with Customers on Social Media

SOCIAL MEDIA PLATFORMS provide an excellent opportunity to engage with your customers directly. Respond to comments, messages, and reviews promptly. Use social media to share valuable content, run contests or giveaways, and create a sense of community around your brand.

8.1.3 Measuring and Evaluating CRM Success

TO ENSURE THE EFFECTIVENESS of your CRM strategies, it is crucial to measure and evaluate their impact. Consider the following metrics:

8.1.3.1 Customer Satisfaction

REGULARLY ASSESS CUSTOMER satisfaction through surveys, feedback forms, or Net Promoter Score (NPS) surveys. Analyze the results to identify areas for improvement and address any issues promptly.

8.1.3.2 Customer Retention Rate

MONITOR YOUR CUSTOMER retention rate to gauge the success of your CRM efforts. A high retention rate indicates that your customers are satisfied and loyal to your brand.

8.1.3.3 Customer Lifetime Value

CALCULATE THE AVERAGE customer lifetime value to understand the long-term profitability of your customer relationships. This metric helps you identify opportunities for upselling, cross-selling, or improving customer loyalty.

8.1.3.4 Customer Referrals

TRACK THE NUMBER OF customer referrals you receive. A high number of referrals indicates that your customers are satisfied and willing to recommend your business to others.

8.1.3.5 Social Media Engagement

MEASURE THE ENGAGEMENT levels on your social media platforms, such as likes, comments, shares, and mentions. Higher engagement indicates that your customers are actively interacting with your brand and content.

8.1.4 Evolving and Adapting CRM Strategies

CRM IS NOT A ONE-TIME effort but an ongoing process. Continuously monitor customer feedback, market trends, and industry developments to adapt and evolve your CRM strategies accordingly. Stay updated with emerging technologies and tools that can enhance your CRM capabilities and provide better customer experiences.

By understanding and implementing effective CRM strategies, you can build strong and lasting relationships with your customers. This not only leads to increased customer satisfaction and loyalty but also drives business growth and success in the competitive online marketplace.

8.2 Building Customer Loyalty

———

B uilding customer loyalty is a crucial aspect of running a successful online business. When you have loyal customers, they not only continue to purchase from you but also become advocates for your brand, spreading positive word-of-mouth and attracting new customers. In this section, we will explore strategies and techniques to build and nurture customer loyalty in the online space.

8.2.1 Understanding the Importance of Customer Loyalty

CUSTOMER LOYALTY IS the result of consistently delivering exceptional products, services, and experiences that meet or exceed customer expectations. Loyal customers are more likely to make repeat purchases, spend more money, and refer others to your business. They also provide valuable feedback and insights that can help you improve your offerings and grow your business.

In the online world, where competition is fierce and customers have numerous options, building customer loyalty becomes even more critical. By focusing on building strong relationships with your customers, you can differentiate yourself from competitors and create a loyal customer base that will support your business in the long run.

8.2.2 Providing Personalized Experiences

ONE EFFECTIVE WAY TO build customer loyalty is by providing personalized experiences. Personalization involves tailoring your products, services, and communications to meet the specific needs and preferences of individual customers. By understanding your customers' preferences, you can create targeted marketing campaigns, recommend relevant products, and provide personalized customer support.

To implement personalization effectively, you can leverage customer data and analytics. By collecting and analyzing data such as purchase history, browsing behavior, and demographic information, you can gain insights into your customers' preferences and behaviors. This information can then be used to deliver personalized experiences that resonate with your customers and make them feel valued.

8.2.3 Building Trust and Transparency

TRUST IS A FUNDAMENTAL element of building customer loyalty. Customers are more likely to remain loyal to a brand they trust. To build trust, it is essential to be transparent in your business practices. This includes being honest about your products and services, pricing, and any potential limitations or risks.

Transparency can be demonstrated through clear and accurate product descriptions, honest customer reviews, and open communication channels. By being transparent, you establish credibility and foster trust with your customers, which in turn leads to increased loyalty.

8.2.4 Rewarding Loyalty

REWARDING LOYAL CUSTOMERS is an effective strategy to encourage repeat purchases and foster long-term loyalty. There are various ways to reward customer loyalty, such as loyalty programs, exclusive discounts, special offers, and personalized incentives.

Loyalty programs can be structured in different ways, such as point-based systems, tiered rewards, or VIP memberships. These programs incentivize customers to continue purchasing from your business by offering exclusive benefits and rewards. By providing tangible rewards for their loyalty, you not only encourage repeat purchases but also make your customers feel appreciated and valued.

8.2.5 Providing Exceptional Customer Service

EXCEPTIONAL CUSTOMER service is a cornerstone of building customer loyalty. When customers have a positive experience with your business, they are more likely to remain loyal and recommend your brand to others. To provide exceptional customer service, it is crucial to be responsive, attentive, and empathetic to your customers' needs.

In the online space, customer service can be delivered through various channels, such as live chat, email, social media, and phone support. It is important to respond promptly to customer inquiries and provide solutions to their problems. By going above and beyond to meet customer expectations, you can create a positive impression and build strong relationships with your customers.

8.2.6 Engaging with Customers

ENGAGING WITH YOUR customers is another effective way to build loyalty. By actively interacting with your customers, you can create a sense of community and foster a deeper connection with your brand. This can be done through various channels, such as social media, email newsletters, blog comments, and online forums.

Engagement can take the form of responding to customer comments and feedback, asking for their opinions and suggestions, and involving them in the decision-making process. By involving your customers in your business, you make them feel valued and part of a larger community, which strengthens their loyalty to your brand.

8.2.7 Monitoring and Responding to Feedback

COLLECTING AND UTILIZING customer feedback is essential for building customer loyalty. By actively seeking feedback from your customers, you can gain valuable insights into their experiences, preferences, and areas for improvement. This feedback can help you identify and address any issues or concerns promptly.

To collect feedback, you can use various methods such as surveys, online reviews, social media listening, and customer support interactions. It is important to monitor feedback regularly and respond promptly and appropriately. By addressing customer concerns and taking action based on their feedback, you demonstrate that you value their opinions and are committed to providing the best possible experience.

8.2.8 Building Long-Term Relationships

BUILDING CUSTOMER LOYALTY is not just about one-time transactions; it is about building long-term relationships with your customers. By focusing on creating meaningful connections and providing ongoing value, you can foster loyalty that extends beyond individual purchases.

To build long-term relationships, it is important to stay in touch with your customers even after the initial sale. This can be done through email newsletters, personalized recommendations, exclusive offers, and regular updates. By nurturing these relationships, you can turn one-time customers into loyal advocates for your brand.

In conclusion, building customer loyalty is a vital aspect of running a successful online business. By providing personalized experiences, building trust, rewarding loyalty, providing exceptional customer service, engaging with customers, monitoring feedback, and building long-term relationships, you can create a loyal customer base that supports your business and helps it thrive in the competitive online landscape.

8.3 Providing Exceptional Customer Service

In the world of online entrepreneurship, providing exceptional customer service is crucial for building a loyal customer base and ensuring the long-term success of your business. When customers have a positive experience with your brand, they are more likely to become repeat customers and recommend your products or services to others. On the other hand, poor customer service can lead to negative reviews, customer dissatisfaction, and ultimately, a decline in sales. Therefore, it is essential to prioritize customer service and go above and beyond to meet and exceed customer expectations.

8.3.1 Understanding the Importance of Customer Service

CUSTOMER SERVICE IS not just about resolving complaints or answering inquiries; it is about creating a positive and memorable experience for your customers. When customers feel valued and appreciated, they are more likely to develop a sense of loyalty towards your brand. Exceptional customer service can differentiate your business from competitors and give you a competitive edge in the market.

Moreover, providing excellent customer service can also lead to increased customer satisfaction and retention. Satisfied customers are more likely to continue doing business with you and become brand advocates, spreading positive word-of-mouth about your products or services.

8.3.2 Building a Customer-Centric Culture

TO PROVIDE EXCEPTIONAL customer service, it is essential to build a customer-centric culture within your organization. This means putting the needs and preferences of your customers at the forefront of your business operations. Here are some strategies to foster a customer-centric culture:

1. **Empower your employees:** Train and empower your employees to make decisions and take actions that prioritize customer satisfaction. Encourage them to go the extra mile to meet customer needs and resolve issues promptly.

2. **Listen to customer feedback:** Actively seek feedback from your customers and use it to improve your products, services, and customer experience. Regularly monitor customer reviews, conduct surveys, and engage in social listening to gain insights into customer preferences and pain points.

3. **Personalize the customer experience:** Tailor your interactions with customers to their specific needs and preferences. Use customer data and analytics to create personalized experiences, such as personalized recommendations, targeted marketing campaigns, and customized offers.

4. **Communicate effectively:** Ensure clear and timely communication with your customers. Be responsive to their inquiries, provide updates on order status or

service requests, and proactively communicate any changes or disruptions that may affect them.

8.3.3 Going Above and Beyond

PROVIDING EXCEPTIONAL customer service goes beyond meeting basic expectations. It involves going above and beyond to surprise and delight your customers. Here are some ways to exceed customer expectations:

1. **Anticipate customer needs:** Proactively identify and address customer needs before they even arise. For example, if you notice a customer frequently purchases a particular product, you can offer a subscription service or send reminders when it's time to reorder.

2. **Offer personalized support:** Provide personalized support to customers by assigning dedicated account managers or customer service representatives. This ensures that customers have a single point of contact who understands their unique needs and can provide tailored assistance.

3. **Provide timely and efficient solutions:** When customers have an issue or complaint, respond promptly and work towards resolving the problem as quickly as possible. Empower your customer service team to make decisions and take actions that prioritize customer satisfaction.

4. **Surprise and delight:** Surprise your customers with unexpected gestures of appreciation. This could be sending personalized thank-you notes, offering

exclusive discounts or rewards, or providing freebies or samples with their purchase.

8.3.4 Leveraging Technology for Customer Service

TECHNOLOGY PLAYS A vital role in delivering exceptional customer service in the digital age. Here are some ways you can leverage technology to enhance your customer service efforts:

1. **Implement a customer relationship management (CRM) system:** A CRM system helps you manage and track customer interactions, preferences, and purchase history. It enables you to provide personalized experiences, track customer inquiries, and streamline customer service processes.

2. **Utilize live chat and chatbots:** Implement live chat functionality on your website to provide real-time support to customers. Additionally, consider using chatbots to automate responses to frequently asked questions and provide instant assistance.

3. **Offer self-service options:** Provide self-service options such as a comprehensive FAQ section, knowledge base, or video tutorials. This allows customers to find answers to their questions or troubleshoot issues on their own, reducing the need for direct customer support.

4. **Monitor social media:** Monitor social media platforms for customer inquiries, feedback, and mentions of your brand. Respond promptly to customer messages and comments, and use social

listening tools to gain insights into customer sentiment and preferences.

8.3.5 Measuring Customer Service Success

TO ENSURE THAT YOU are providing exceptional customer service, it is important to measure and track your performance. Here are some key metrics to consider:

1. **Customer satisfaction (CSAT) score:** Measure customer satisfaction by conducting surveys or using post-purchase feedback tools. This metric provides insights into how satisfied your customers are with your products, services, and overall experience.
2. **Net Promoter Score (NPS):** NPS measures customer loyalty and their likelihood to recommend your brand to others. It is calculated based on a single question: "On a scale of 0-10, how likely are you to recommend our company/product/service to a friend or colleague?"
3. **First response time:** Measure the average time it takes for your customer service team to respond to customer inquiries or complaints. Aim to minimize this time to ensure timely support.
4. **Resolution time:** Track the average time it takes to resolve customer issues or complaints. Strive to reduce this time while still providing effective solutions.

By regularly monitoring these metrics, you can identify areas for improvement and make data-driven decisions to enhance your customer service efforts.

Remember, exceptional customer service is not a one-time effort but an ongoing commitment. Continuously strive to improve and adapt your customer service strategies to meet the evolving needs and expectations of your customers. By providing exceptional customer service, you can build strong customer relationships, foster loyalty, and ultimately drive the success of your online business.

8.4 Collecting and Utilizing Customer Feedback

Customer feedback is a valuable resource for any online entrepreneur. It provides insights into the needs, preferences, and satisfaction levels of your target audience. By collecting and utilizing customer feedback effectively, you can make informed decisions, improve your products or services, and enhance the overall customer experience. In this section, we will explore the importance of collecting customer feedback, different methods to gather feedback, and how to leverage this information to drive business growth.

8.4.1 The Importance of Collecting Customer Feedback

COLLECTING CUSTOMER feedback is crucial for several reasons. Firstly, it helps you understand your customers better. By listening to their opinions, suggestions, and concerns, you gain valuable insights into their needs and expectations. This knowledge allows you to tailor your products or services to meet their specific requirements, ultimately increasing customer satisfaction and loyalty.

Secondly, customer feedback provides you with a competitive advantage. By staying attuned to your customers' preferences and staying ahead of industry trends, you can differentiate yourself from your competitors. This allows you to offer unique and innovative solutions that resonate with your target audience, giving you a competitive edge in the market.

Lastly, customer feedback serves as a tool for continuous improvement. By identifying areas for improvement and addressing customer pain points, you can refine your offerings and enhance the overall customer experience. This iterative process of feedback collection and improvement enables you to stay relevant and adapt to changing customer needs, ensuring the long-term success of your online business.

8.4.2 Methods of Collecting Customer Feedback

THERE ARE VARIOUS METHODS you can use to collect customer feedback. Here are some effective approaches:

Surveys and Questionnaires

SURVEYS AND QUESTIONNAIRES are a popular and efficient way to gather customer feedback. You can create online surveys using platforms like Google Forms or SurveyMonkey and distribute them to your target audience via email, social media, or your website. Make sure your questions are clear, concise, and relevant to gather meaningful insights. Consider offering incentives, such as discounts or freebies, to encourage participation.

Customer Reviews and Ratings

CUSTOMER REVIEWS AND ratings are a powerful form of feedback that can influence purchasing decisions. Encourage your customers to leave reviews on your website, social media platforms, or third-party review sites. Monitor and respond to these reviews promptly, whether they are positive or negative. This shows your customers that you value their feedback and are committed to addressing their concerns.

Social Media Listening

SOCIAL MEDIA PLATFORMS provide a wealth of information about your customers' opinions and experiences. Monitor social media channels for mentions of your brand, products, or services. Pay attention to both direct mentions and indirect conversations related to your industry. This real-time feedback can help you identify emerging trends, address customer issues, and engage with your audience more effectively.

Customer Interviews and Focus Groups

IN-DEPTH INTERVIEWS and focus groups allow you to gather detailed feedback from a select group of customers. This qualitative approach provides deeper insights into their experiences, motivations, and pain points. Consider offering incentives, such as gift cards or exclusive access, to encourage participation. Conduct these interviews in person, over the phone, or through video conferencing platforms.

Website Analytics

WEBSITE ANALYTICS TOOLS, such as Google Analytics, can provide valuable data on customer behavior and preferences. Analyze metrics like page views, bounce rates, and conversion rates to understand how customers interact with your website. This data can help you identify areas for improvement and optimize the user experience.

8.4.3 Leveraging Customer Feedback for Business Growth

COLLECTING CUSTOMER feedback is only the first step. To drive business growth, you must effectively utilize this feedback. Here are some strategies to leverage customer feedback:

Identify Patterns and Trends

ANALYZE THE FEEDBACK you receive to identify common patterns and trends. Look for recurring themes, issues, or suggestions that can guide your decision-making process. This analysis will help you prioritize areas for improvement and focus on the most impactful changes.

Act on Feedback

TAKE ACTION BASED ON the feedback you receive. Address customer concerns, implement suggested improvements, and make necessary changes to your products, services, or processes. Communicate these changes to your customers to show that you value their feedback and are committed to their satisfaction.

Engage with Customers

ENGAGE WITH YOUR CUSTOMERS throughout the feedback process. Respond to their feedback promptly and transparently. Show appreciation for their input and keep them informed about any actions you take as a result of their feedback. This engagement builds trust and strengthens the relationship between your brand and your customers.

Use Feedback for Marketing and Sales

LEVERAGE POSITIVE CUSTOMER feedback in your marketing and sales efforts. Highlight testimonials, reviews, and ratings on your website, social media platforms, and marketing materials. This social proof can build credibility and trust with potential customers, increasing the likelihood of conversions.

Continuously Improve

CUSTOMER FEEDBACK SHOULD be an ongoing process. Regularly collect feedback, analyze it, and make improvements accordingly. Embrace a culture of continuous improvement within your organization, and encourage all team members to actively seek and utilize customer feedback.

By collecting and utilizing customer feedback effectively, you can gain a deeper understanding of your target audience, improve your products or services, and foster long-term customer loyalty. Embrace the power of customer feedback as a catalyst for growth and success in your online entrepreneurship journey.

Conclusion

———

Collecting and utilizing customer feedback is a vital component of building a successful online business. By actively listening to your customers, you can gain valuable insights, improve your offerings, and enhance the overall customer experience. Implementing effective feedback collection methods and leveraging this information for business growth will set you apart from your competitors and ensure the long-term success of your online venture. Embrace the power of customer feedback and let it guide you on your path to digital success.

Continuous Learning and Personal Development

9.1 Embracing a Growth Mindset

———

I n the ever-evolving world of online entrepreneurship, one of the most crucial factors for success is the mindset of the entrepreneur. A growth mindset is the foundation upon which all other skills and strategies are built. It is the belief that abilities and intelligence can be developed through dedication, hard work, and a willingness to learn from failures and setbacks. Embracing a growth mindset is essential for online entrepreneurs as it allows them to adapt to challenges, overcome obstacles, and continuously improve their skills and knowledge.

9.1.1 The Power of a Growth Mindset

A GROWTH MINDSET IS a powerful tool that can transform the way you approach your online business. It enables you to see failures and setbacks as opportunities for growth and learning, rather than as indicators of your abilities or potential. With a growth mindset, you understand that success is not solely determined by innate talent or intelligence but is instead a result of effort, perseverance, and a willingness to learn from mistakes.

By embracing a growth mindset, you open yourself up to new possibilities and opportunities. You become more resilient in the face of challenges and setbacks, as you understand that they are not permanent roadblocks but temporary obstacles that can be overcome with the right mindset and approach. A growth mindset allows you to view failures as valuable learning experiences and to use them as stepping stones towards success.

9.1.2 Cultivating a Growth Mindset

CULTIVATING A GROWTH mindset requires a conscious effort and a commitment to personal growth and development. Here are some strategies to help you embrace a growth mindset as an online entrepreneur:

9.1.2.1 Embrace Challenges

INSTEAD OF SHYING AWAY from challenges, embrace them as opportunities for growth. Challenges push you out of your comfort zone and force you to develop new skills and strategies. Embracing challenges allows you to expand your capabilities and become a more effective and adaptable entrepreneur.

9.1.2.2 Learn from Failure

FAILURE IS AN INEVITABLE part of the entrepreneurial journey. Instead of viewing failure as a reflection of your abilities or potential, see it as a valuable learning experience. Analyze your failures, identify the lessons they offer, and use them to improve your strategies and decision-making.

9.1.2.3 Seek Feedback and Criticism

FEEDBACK AND CRITICISM are invaluable tools for growth and improvement. Embrace feedback from customers, mentors, and peers, and use it to refine your products, services, and strategies. Be open to constructive criticism and view it as an opportunity to learn and grow.

9.1.2.4 Develop a Learning Mindset

APPROACH EVERY EXPERIENCE and interaction as an opportunity to learn. Continuously seek out new knowledge, skills, and perspectives. Invest in your education and skill development by attending workshops, webinars, and conferences, and by reading books and articles related to your industry.

9.1.2.5 Surround Yourself with Like-Minded Individuals

SURROUNDING YOURSELF with like-minded individuals who share your passion for growth and learning can be incredibly beneficial. Join online communities, attend networking events, and seek out mentors and peers who can support and inspire you on your entrepreneurial journey.

9.1.3 Overcoming Limiting Beliefs

ONE OF THE BIGGEST obstacles to embracing a growth mindset is the presence of limiting beliefs. These are negative thoughts and beliefs that hold you back from reaching your full potential. Common limiting beliefs include thoughts such as "I'm not good enough," "I don't have what it takes," or "I'm not smart enough."

To overcome limiting beliefs, it is important to challenge and reframe them. Replace negative thoughts with positive affirmations and focus on your strengths and accomplishments. Surround yourself with positive influences and seek out evidence that contradicts your limiting beliefs. By consciously challenging and reframing your limiting beliefs, you can create a more empowering and growth-oriented mindset.

9.1.4 The Benefits of a Growth Mindset

EMBRACING A GROWTH mindset as an online entrepreneur offers numerous benefits. Here are some of the key advantages:

9.1.4.1 Increased Resilience

A GROWTH MINDSET ALLOWS you to bounce back from failures and setbacks more quickly and effectively. It enables you to view challenges as opportunities for growth and to persevere in the face of adversity.

9.1.4.2 Continuous Learning and Improvement

WITH A GROWTH MINDSET, you are constantly seeking out new knowledge and skills. This commitment to learning and improvement allows you to stay ahead of industry trends, adapt to changes, and continuously refine your strategies and approaches.

9.1.4.3 Greater Creativity and Innovation

A GROWTH MINDSET ENCOURAGES you to think outside the box and explore new ideas and possibilities. It fosters a sense of curiosity and a willingness to take risks, leading to greater creativity and innovation in your online business.

9.1.4.4 Increased Confidence

AS YOU EMBRACE A GROWTH mindset and witness your own growth and progress, your confidence will naturally increase. You will develop a belief in your ability to overcome challenges and achieve your goals, which will propel you forward on your entrepreneurial journey.

Conclusion

EMBRACING A GROWTH mindset is essential for online entrepreneurs who want to thrive in the ever-changing digital landscape. By cultivating a growth mindset, you can overcome challenges, learn from failures, and continuously improve your skills and knowledge. With a growth mindset, you have the power to transform obstacles into opportunities and to achieve long-term success in your online business.

9.2 Investing in Education and Skill Development

———

As an online entrepreneur, investing in education and skill development is crucial for your long-term success. The digital landscape is constantly evolving, and staying ahead of the curve requires continuous learning and personal growth. By investing in your education and developing new skills, you can enhance your expertise, adapt to industry changes, and seize new opportunities. In this section, we will explore the importance of investing in education and skill development and provide practical strategies to help you stay ahead in the ever-changing online business world.

9.2.1 The Value of Lifelong Learning

IN THE FAST-PACED DIGITAL era, knowledge becomes obsolete quickly. To remain competitive, you must embrace a mindset of lifelong learning. Continuous education not only expands your knowledge base but also enhances your problem-solving abilities, critical thinking skills, and creativity. By investing in your education, you can gain a deeper understanding of your industry, identify emerging trends, and make informed decisions for your online business.

9.2.2 Identifying Skill Gaps

BEFORE YOU CAN INVEST in education and skill development, it's essential to identify your skill gaps. Reflect on your strengths and weaknesses as an online entrepreneur. Are there specific areas where you lack expertise or feel less confident? These skill gaps can be in areas such as digital marketing, website development, financial management, or customer relationship management. Once you have identified your skill gaps, you can prioritize which areas to focus on and develop a plan for acquiring the necessary knowledge and skills.

9.2.3 Formal Education vs. Self-Learning

WHEN IT COMES TO EDUCATION and skill development, you have two main options: formal education and self-learning. Formal education includes pursuing a degree, diploma, or certification program related to your field of interest. This option provides structured learning, access to expert instructors, and the opportunity to network with peers. However, formal education can be time-consuming and expensive.

On the other hand, self-learning allows you to acquire knowledge and skills at your own pace and on your own terms. With the abundance of online resources, you can access tutorials, e-books, webinars, and online courses to enhance your skills. Self-learning offers flexibility and affordability, but it requires self-discipline and motivation to stay committed to your learning journey.

9.2.4 Strategies for Skill Development

REGARDLESS OF WHETHER you choose formal education or self-learning, here are some strategies to help you effectively develop your skills as an online entrepreneur:

9.2.4.1 Online Courses and Webinars

ONLINE COURSES AND webinars are excellent resources for acquiring new skills and knowledge. Many reputable platforms offer courses specifically designed for online entrepreneurs. These courses cover a wide range of topics, including digital marketing, website development, e-commerce, and business management. Look for courses taught by industry experts and read reviews to ensure the quality and relevance of the content.

9.2.4.2 Industry Conferences and Workshops

ATTENDING INDUSTRY conferences and workshops is a great way to stay updated with the latest trends and network with like-minded professionals. These events often feature keynote speakers, panel discussions, and interactive sessions that provide valuable insights and practical tips. Take advantage of networking opportunities to connect with industry leaders and potential collaborators.

9.2.4.3 Mentorship and Coaching

SEEKING MENTORSHIP or coaching from experienced entrepreneurs can accelerate your learning and growth. A mentor or coach can provide guidance, share their experiences, and help you navigate challenges in your online business journey. Look for mentors who have achieved success in your desired field and are willing to invest their time and knowledge in your development.

9.2.4.4 Online Communities and Forums

JOINING ONLINE COMMUNITIES and forums allows you to connect with fellow entrepreneurs, share knowledge, and seek advice. These communities provide a platform for discussions, collaboration, and learning from others' experiences. Engage actively in these communities, ask questions, and contribute your expertise to foster meaningful connections and expand your knowledge base.

9.2.5 Continuous Skill Enhancement

INVESTING IN EDUCATION and skill development is not a one-time effort. To stay relevant in the ever-evolving online business landscape, you must commit to continuous skill enhancement. Set aside dedicated time each week or month to learn and practice new skills. Stay updated with industry news, subscribe to relevant blogs and newsletters, and follow thought leaders on social media. Embrace a growth mindset and view every challenge as an opportunity to learn and grow.

9.2.6 Measuring the Impact of Education and Skill Development

TO ENSURE THAT YOUR investment in education and skill development is paying off, it's essential to measure its impact. Set specific goals related to the skills you want to develop and track your progress over time. Monitor key performance indicators (KPIs) such as increased website traffic, higher conversion rates, improved customer satisfaction, or enhanced financial management. Regularly evaluate the outcomes of your learning efforts and make adjustments as needed.

9.2.7 Conclusion

INVESTING IN EDUCATION and skill development is a fundamental aspect of being a successful online entrepreneur. By continuously learning and enhancing your skills, you can adapt to industry changes, seize new opportunities, and stay ahead of the competition. Whether through formal education or self-learning, make a commitment to lifelong learning and embrace the transformative power of education. Remember, the more you invest in yourself, the greater your chances of achieving long-term success in the dynamic world of online entrepreneurship.

9.3 Networking and Collaboration

―――――

Networking and collaboration are essential components of success in the online business world. As an online entrepreneur, it is crucial to build connections, foster relationships, and collaborate with others in your industry. These activities can open doors to new opportunities, provide valuable insights, and help you stay updated with the latest industry trends. In this section, we will explore the importance of networking and collaboration and provide practical tips on how to leverage these strategies to enhance your online business.

9.3.1 The Power of Networking

NETWORKING IS THE PROCESS of establishing and nurturing relationships with individuals who can potentially support and contribute to your business growth. It involves connecting with like-minded entrepreneurs, industry experts, potential customers, and other professionals in your field. Here are some reasons why networking is crucial for online entrepreneurs:

Building a Supportive Network

NETWORKING ALLOWS YOU to build a supportive network of individuals who understand the challenges and opportunities of the online business world. By connecting with fellow entrepreneurs, you can share experiences, seek advice, and gain valuable insights that can help you overcome obstacles and make informed decisions.

Collaboration and Partnership Opportunities

NETWORKING OPENS DOORS to collaboration and partnership opportunities. By connecting with individuals who complement your skills and expertise, you can explore joint ventures, co-create products or services, and tap into new markets. Collaborating with others can expand your reach, enhance your offerings, and accelerate your business growth.

Access to Resources and Expertise

NETWORKING PROVIDES access to a wide range of resources and expertise. By connecting with industry experts, you can tap into their knowledge, learn from their experiences, and gain insights into industry best practices. Additionally, networking can help you access funding opportunities, mentorship programs, and other resources that can support your business growth.

Building Your Personal Brand

NETWORKING ALLOWS YOU to build your personal brand and establish yourself as an authority in your industry. By actively participating in industry events, conferences, and online communities, you can showcase your expertise, share valuable insights, and gain visibility among your target audience. Building a strong personal brand can attract potential customers, partners, and opportunities for collaboration.

9.3.2 Effective Networking Strategies

NOW THAT WE UNDERSTAND the importance of networking, let's explore some effective strategies to maximize your networking efforts:

Attend Industry Events and Conferences

INDUSTRY EVENTS AND conferences provide excellent opportunities to network with like-minded individuals and industry experts. Make it a point to attend relevant events both online and offline. Engage in conversations, participate in panel discussions, and actively seek out networking opportunities during these events. Remember to exchange contact information and follow up with the individuals you meet to nurture the relationship.

Join Online Communities and Forums

ONLINE COMMUNITIES and forums focused on your industry or niche are great platforms for networking. Participate in discussions, share your expertise, and engage with other members. By actively contributing to these communities, you can build relationships, gain visibility, and establish yourself as a valuable member of the community.

Utilize Social Media Platforms

SOCIAL MEDIA PLATFORMS such as LinkedIn, Twitter, and Facebook can be powerful tools for networking. Connect with professionals in your industry, join relevant groups, and actively engage with their content. Share valuable insights, participate in discussions, and offer support to others. Social media platforms provide a convenient way to network and build relationships with individuals from around the world.

Seek Mentorship and Coaching

MENTORSHIP AND COACHING programs can provide invaluable guidance and support in your entrepreneurial journey. Seek out mentors who have achieved success in your industry and learn from their experiences. They can provide insights, offer advice, and help you navigate challenges. Additionally, consider joining mastermind groups or coaching programs where you can network with other entrepreneurs and receive guidance from experts.

Offer Value and Be Genuine

WHEN NETWORKING, IT is essential to approach relationships with a genuine desire to help and add value. Be proactive in offering assistance, sharing resources, and connecting individuals who can benefit from each other. By being genuine and helpful, you can build trust and establish long-lasting relationships that can contribute to your business growth.

9.3.3 Collaboration for Business Growth

COLLABORATION IS A powerful strategy for business growth. By partnering with others, you can leverage their expertise, resources, and networks to achieve mutual success. Here are some ways you can collaborate with others:

Joint Ventures and Partnerships

CONSIDER FORMING JOINT ventures or partnerships with individuals or businesses that complement your offerings. By combining your strengths, you can create innovative products or services, tap into new markets, and reach a wider audience. Joint ventures and partnerships can provide access to new customers, increase brand visibility, and drive business growth.

Guest Blogging and Content Collaboration

COLLABORATING WITH other bloggers or content creators in your industry can help you expand your reach and attract new audiences. Guest blogging on reputable websites or inviting guest bloggers to contribute to your blog can expose your brand to a wider audience. Additionally, consider collaborating on content creation projects such as ebooks, webinars, or podcasts to provide valuable insights to your target audience.

Cross-Promotion and Referral Programs

COLLABORATE WITH COMPLEMENTARY businesses to cross-promote each other's products or services. By recommending each other to your respective audiences, you can tap into new customer bases and increase brand visibility. Consider setting up referral programs where you reward customers or partners for referring new business to each other.

Co-Creation and Product Development

COLLABORATE WITH OTHER entrepreneurs or businesses to co-create products or services. By pooling your resources, expertise, and ideas, you can develop innovative offerings that cater to a broader market. Co-creation can lead to unique value propositions, increased customer satisfaction, and enhanced competitiveness in the market.

Conclusion

NETWORKING AND COLLABORATION are essential strategies for online entrepreneurs looking to grow their businesses. By actively engaging in networking activities, you can build a supportive network, access valuable resources, and open doors to collaboration opportunities. Collaboration, on the other hand, allows you to leverage the expertise and resources of others to achieve mutual success. By implementing effective networking and collaboration strategies, you can enhance your online presence, expand your reach, and accelerate your business growth. Embrace the power of networking and collaboration, and unlock the full potential of your online venture.

9.4 Staying Updated with Industry Trends

———

In the fast-paced world of online entrepreneurship, staying updated with industry trends is crucial for success. The digital landscape is constantly evolving, and new technologies, strategies, and consumer behaviors emerge regularly. As an online entrepreneur, it is essential to stay ahead of the curve and adapt to these changes to remain competitive and relevant in your industry.

9.4.1 Importance of Industry Trends

UNDERSTANDING AND STAYING updated with industry trends provides several benefits for online entrepreneurs. Here are a few reasons why it is important to keep a pulse on the latest developments in your field:

1. Identifying Opportunities

BY STAYING UPDATED with industry trends, you can identify new opportunities for growth and innovation. Trends often indicate emerging markets, consumer demands, and gaps in the market that you can leverage to your advantage. By being aware of these opportunities, you can position your business strategically and capitalize on them before your competitors.

2. Anticipating Customer Needs

INDUSTRY TRENDS OFTEN reflect changes in consumer behavior and preferences. By staying updated, you can anticipate the evolving needs and expectations of your target audience. This knowledge allows you to tailor your products, services, and marketing strategies to meet those needs effectively. By staying ahead of your customers' expectations, you can build stronger relationships and maintain a competitive edge.

3. Adapting to Technological Advancements

TECHNOLOGY PLAYS A significant role in shaping industry trends. New tools, platforms, and innovations can disrupt traditional business models and create new opportunities. By staying updated with technological advancements, you can leverage these tools to streamline your operations, improve efficiency, and enhance the customer experience. Embracing new technologies can give you a competitive advantage and help you stay ahead of your competitors.

4. Enhancing Decision-Making

STAYING UPDATED WITH industry trends provides you with valuable insights and data that can inform your decision-making process. By understanding the current state of your industry, you can make informed choices about product development, marketing strategies, and business expansion.

This knowledge reduces the risk of making uninformed decisions and increases the likelihood of success.

9.4.2 Sources of Industry Trends

TO STAY UPDATED WITH industry trends, it is essential to have reliable sources of information. Here are some sources you can utilize:

1. Industry Publications and Websites

INDUSTRY-SPECIFIC PUBLICATIONS and websites are excellent sources of information for staying updated with trends. These publications often provide in-depth analysis, case studies, and expert opinions on the latest developments in your field. Subscribing to newsletters, following industry blogs, and joining relevant forums can help you access valuable insights and stay informed.

2. Social Media

SOCIAL MEDIA PLATFORMS are not only for connecting with your audience but also for staying updated with industry trends. Follow thought leaders, industry influencers, and relevant hashtags to get real-time updates on the latest news, trends, and discussions in your industry. Engaging in conversations and networking with professionals in your field can also provide valuable insights.

3. Industry Events and Conferences

ATTENDING INDUSTRY events and conferences is an excellent way to stay updated with the latest trends. These events often feature keynote speakers, panel discussions, and workshops that provide valuable insights into the current state of your industry. Networking with other professionals and exchanging ideas can also help you stay ahead of the curve.

4. Market Research and Reports

MARKET RESEARCH AND reports provide valuable data and insights into industry trends. These reports often include market analysis, consumer behavior trends, and future projections. By studying these reports, you can gain a deeper understanding of your industry and make informed decisions based on data-driven insights.

9.4.3 Implementing Industry Trends

STAYING UPDATED WITH industry trends is not enough; you must also implement them effectively in your business. Here are some tips for implementing industry trends:

1. Evaluate Relevance

NOT ALL INDUSTRY TRENDS will be relevant to your business. Evaluate each trend and assess its potential impact on your business goals and target audience. Focus on trends that align with your vision, mission, and values.

2. Plan and Strategize

ONCE YOU HAVE IDENTIFIED relevant trends, develop a plan and strategy for implementing them. Determine how each trend can be integrated into your existing business model, products, services, or marketing strategies. Set clear goals and objectives for each implementation.

3. Test and Measure

BEFORE FULLY IMPLEMENTING a trend, test it on a smaller scale to assess its effectiveness. Use analytics and data to measure the impact of the trend on your business. Make adjustments and improvements based on the results.

4. Stay Agile

THE DIGITAL LANDSCAPE is dynamic, and trends can change rapidly. Stay agile and adaptable to embrace new trends and adjust your strategies accordingly. Continuously monitor industry developments and be ready to pivot when necessary.

Conclusion

STAYING UPDATED WITH industry trends is essential for online entrepreneurs to remain competitive and relevant in the digital business landscape. By understanding the importance of industry trends, utilizing reliable sources of information, and effectively implementing trends in your business, you can position yourself for long-term success. Embrace the ever-changing nature of the online world and use industry trends as a compass to navigate your path to digital success.

Navigating Challenges and Embracing Success

10.1 Overcoming Common Online Business Challenges

———

S tarting and running an online business can be an exciting and rewarding endeavor. However, it is not without its challenges. In this section, we will explore some of the common challenges that online entrepreneurs face and discuss strategies for overcoming them.

10.1.1 Dealing with Competition

ONE OF THE BIGGEST challenges in the online business landscape is the presence of competition. With millions of websites and online businesses vying for attention, standing out from the crowd can be difficult. To overcome this challenge, it is important to differentiate your business and offer something unique to your target audience.

Start by conducting thorough market research to identify gaps or unmet needs in your industry. This will allow you to position your business in a way that sets it apart from competitors. Focus on providing value and delivering exceptional customer experiences to build a loyal customer base.

Additionally, stay updated with industry trends and constantly innovate to stay ahead of the competition. Embrace change and be willing to adapt your strategies and offerings to meet evolving customer demands.

10.1.2 Building Trust and Credibility

ESTABLISHING TRUST and credibility is crucial for the success of any online business. However, it can be challenging to build trust with potential customers who may be skeptical of doing business online. To overcome this challenge, focus on building a strong online presence and showcasing your expertise.

Invest in creating a professional website that is user-friendly and visually appealing. Provide clear and transparent information about your products or services, including pricing, shipping, and return policies. Incorporate customer testimonials and reviews to demonstrate social proof and build trust.

Engage with your audience through social media platforms and online communities. Respond to customer inquiries promptly and provide helpful and informative content. By consistently delivering value and demonstrating your expertise, you can establish yourself as a trusted authority in your industry.

10.1.3 Managing Cash Flow

CASH FLOW MANAGEMENT is a critical aspect of running any business, and online businesses are no exception. It can be challenging to maintain a steady cash flow, especially in the early stages when expenses may outweigh revenue. To overcome this challenge, it is important to develop a solid financial plan and implement effective budgeting strategies.

Start by creating a detailed budget that outlines your expected income and expenses. Monitor your cash flow regularly and identify areas where you can reduce costs or increase revenue. Consider implementing strategies such as offering discounts for early payment or implementing a subscription-based model to generate recurring revenue.

Additionally, establish relationships with reliable suppliers and negotiate favorable payment terms. This can help you manage your inventory and reduce the risk of cash flow issues due to delayed payments or unexpected expenses.

10.1.4 Adapting to Technological Advancements

THE ONLINE BUSINESS landscape is constantly evolving, with new technologies and platforms emerging regularly. Adapting to these technological advancements can be a challenge, but it is essential for the long-term success of your online business.

Stay updated with industry trends and invest in continuous learning and skill development. Attend webinars, workshops, and conferences to stay informed about the latest technologies and best practices in your industry. Network with other online entrepreneurs and collaborate on projects to leverage collective knowledge and expertise.

Embrace automation and leverage technology to streamline your business processes. Implement tools and software that can help you automate repetitive tasks, manage customer relationships, and analyze data. By staying ahead of technological advancements, you can position your business for growth and remain competitive in the online marketplace.

10.1.5 Balancing Work and Personal Life

RUNNING AN ONLINE BUSINESS can be demanding, and finding a balance between work and personal life can be a challenge. It is easy to get consumed by the demands of your business and neglect other aspects of your life. However, maintaining a healthy work-life balance is crucial for your overall well-being and the long-term success of your business.

Set clear boundaries and establish a schedule that allows for dedicated time for work, personal activities, and relaxation. Prioritize self-care and make time for activities that recharge and rejuvenate you. Delegate tasks and outsource non-core activities to free up your time and focus on strategic aspects of your business.

Remember that achieving success is a journey, and it is important to celebrate milestones and achievements along the way. Take time to acknowledge and reward yourself for your hard work and accomplishments. This will help you stay motivated and maintain a positive mindset as you navigate the challenges of running an online business.

In conclusion, while online entrepreneurship comes with its fair share of challenges, with the right mindset and strategies, you can overcome them and achieve success. By differentiating your business, building trust and credibility, managing cash flow effectively, adapting to technological advancements, and maintaining a healthy work-life balance, you can navigate the challenges of the online business landscape and thrive in the digital world.

10.2 Adapting to Technological Advancements

In the fast-paced world of online entrepreneurship, staying ahead of technological advancements is crucial for long-term success. Technology is constantly evolving, and as an online entrepreneur, it is essential to adapt and embrace these advancements to remain competitive and relevant in the digital marketplace. This section will explore the importance of adapting to technological advancements and provide strategies for incorporating new technologies into your online business.

10.2.1 Embracing Change

TECHNOLOGICAL ADVANCEMENTS have the power to revolutionize industries and disrupt traditional business models. As an online entrepreneur, it is important to embrace change and view technological advancements as opportunities rather than threats. By staying informed about emerging technologies and trends, you can position yourself to take advantage of new opportunities and stay ahead of the competition.

10.2.2 Continuous Learning

TO ADAPT TO TECHNOLOGICAL advancements, continuous learning is essential. As an online entrepreneur, you must be willing to invest time and effort into learning about new technologies and how they can benefit your business. This may involve attending industry conferences, participating in online courses, or joining professional networks to stay updated with the latest trends and developments.

10.2.3 Research and Analysis

BEFORE INCORPORATING new technologies into your online business, it is important to conduct thorough research and analysis. This will help you understand the potential benefits and risks associated with adopting new technologies. Consider factors such as cost, compatibility with existing systems, and the impact on your target audience. By conducting proper research and analysis, you can make informed decisions about which technologies to embrace and how to integrate them into your business.

10.2.4 Collaboration and Partnerships

ADAPTING TO TECHNOLOGICAL advancements can be challenging, especially if you do not have the necessary expertise or resources. In such cases, collaboration and partnerships can be valuable. Seek out experts or technology providers who can assist you in implementing new technologies and provide guidance throughout the process. Collaborating with others can help you leverage their knowledge and experience, making the transition smoother and more successful.

10.2.5 Test and Iterate

WHEN INCORPORATING new technologies into your online business, it is important to test and iterate. Start with small-scale implementations and gather feedback from your target audience. This will allow you to identify any issues or areas for improvement before fully integrating the technology into your business operations. By testing and iterating, you can ensure that the technology aligns with your business goals and provides a positive user experience.

10.2.6 Automation and Efficiency

TECHNOLOGICAL ADVANCEMENTS often bring opportunities for automation and increased efficiency. Look for ways to automate repetitive tasks and streamline your business processes using new technologies. This can free up time and resources, allowing you to focus on more strategic activities that drive growth and innovation. Embracing automation and efficiency can give you a competitive edge in the online marketplace.

10.2.7 Data-Driven Decision Making

TECHNOLOGICAL ADVANCEMENTS have also led to an abundance of data available to online entrepreneurs. By harnessing the power of data analytics, you can make informed decisions and optimize your business strategies. Implement tools and systems that allow you to collect, analyze, and interpret data related to your online business. This will enable you to identify trends, understand customer behavior, and make data-driven decisions that drive business growth.

10.2.8 Cybersecurity and Privacy

AS TECHNOLOGY ADVANCES, so do the risks associated with cybersecurity and privacy. It is crucial for online entrepreneurs to prioritize cybersecurity measures to protect their business and customer data. Stay updated with the latest cybersecurity threats and invest in robust security systems and protocols. Additionally, ensure that you comply with privacy regulations and prioritize the protection of your customers' personal information.

10.2.9 Future-Proofing Your Business

TECHNOLOGICAL ADVANCEMENTS are constantly evolving, and it is important to future-proof your online business. Stay informed about emerging technologies and trends that may impact your industry. Continuously evaluate and update your business strategies to align with the changing technological landscape. By staying proactive and adaptable, you can position your business for long-term success in the ever-changing digital marketplace.

In conclusion, adapting to technological advancements is essential for online entrepreneurs to stay competitive and relevant in the digital marketplace. By embracing change, continuously learning, conducting research and analysis, collaborating with others, testing and iterating, automating processes, making data-driven decisions, prioritizing cybersecurity, and future-proofing your business, you can successfully incorporate new technologies into your online venture. Embrace the opportunities that technological advancements bring and position yourself for long-term success in the dynamic world of online entrepreneurship.

10.3 Celebrating Milestones and Achievements

―――

A s an online entrepreneur, it's important to take the time to celebrate your milestones and achievements along the way. Building a successful online business is no easy feat, and acknowledging your progress and accomplishments can provide a much-needed boost of motivation and inspiration. In this section, we will explore the importance of celebrating milestones, different ways to commemorate your achievements, and how to use these celebrations as a springboard for continued success.

10.3.1 Recognizing the Importance of Celebrating Milestones

CELEBRATING MILESTONES and achievements is crucial for several reasons. Firstly, it allows you to reflect on how far you've come and the progress you've made. It's easy to get caught up in the day-to-day challenges of running an online business and lose sight of the bigger picture. By taking the time to celebrate milestones, you can gain a renewed sense of perspective and appreciation for your journey.

Secondly, celebrating milestones helps to boost morale and motivation. Entrepreneurship can be a lonely and demanding path, and it's important to acknowledge and reward yourself for your hard work and dedication. Celebrating milestones can provide a much-needed morale boost during challenging times and serve as a reminder of your ability to overcome obstacles.

Lastly, celebrating milestones can also inspire and motivate others. As an online entrepreneur, you have the opportunity to influence and inspire others who are on a similar path. By openly celebrating your achievements, you can show others what is possible and encourage them to pursue their own entrepreneurial dreams.

10.3.2 Different Ways to Celebrate Milestones and Achievements

THERE ARE NUMEROUS ways to celebrate milestones and achievements in your online business. The key is to choose methods that resonate with you and align with your values and preferences. Here are a few ideas to get you started:

1. Reflect and Appreciate

TAKE SOME TIME TO REFLECT on your journey and appreciate the progress you've made. Write in a journal or create a gratitude list, highlighting the milestones you've achieved and the lessons you've learned along the way. This simple act of reflection can be incredibly powerful in recognizing and celebrating your achievements.

2. Share Your Success

SHARE YOUR MILESTONES and achievements with your online community. Whether it's through a blog post, social media update, or newsletter, let your audience know about your progress and how you've reached a significant milestone. Not only does this allow you to celebrate, but it also helps to build credibility and inspire others.

3. Treat Yourself

REWARD YOURSELF FOR reaching a milestone. Treat yourself to something special, whether it's a small indulgence like a spa day or a larger reward like a vacation. The important thing is to acknowledge your hard work and give yourself a well-deserved break or treat.

4. Host a Celebration Event

CONSIDER HOSTING A celebration event to commemorate a major milestone. This could be a virtual gathering with your online community, a webinar or workshop sharing your journey and lessons learned, or even a physical event if it aligns with your business model. Celebrating with others can create a sense of camaraderie and shared success.

5. Collaborate and Give Back

USE YOUR MILESTONE as an opportunity to collaborate with others and give back to your community. For example, you could partner with a charity or nonprofit organization and donate a portion of your profits to a cause you care about. This not only celebrates your achievement but also allows you to make a positive impact in the world.

10.3.3 Using Milestone Celebrations as a Springboard for Continued Success

WHILE CELEBRATING MILESTONES is important, it's equally crucial to use these celebrations as a springboard for continued success. Here are a few ways to leverage your achievements for future growth:

1. Reflect on Lessons Learned

TAKE THE TIME TO REFLECT on the lessons you've learned from reaching a milestone. What strategies or actions contributed to your success? What challenges did you overcome? By analyzing your achievements, you can identify valuable insights that can inform your future decisions and actions.

2. Set New Goals

ONCE YOU'VE CELEBRATED a milestone, it's time to set new goals and aspirations for your online business. Use your achievements as a launching pad for even greater success. Set ambitious yet attainable goals that will challenge you to grow and push the boundaries of what you thought was possible.

3. Share Your Journey

CONTINUE TO SHARE YOUR journey and progress with your online community. By openly discussing your achievements and challenges, you can inspire and motivate others who are on a similar path. Additionally, sharing your experiences can help you build credibility and establish yourself as an authority in your niche.

4. Stay Humble and Grateful

AS YOU CELEBRATE YOUR milestones, it's important to stay humble and grateful. Remember that success is a result of hard work, dedication, and the support of others. Express gratitude to your team, mentors, and customers who have played a role in your achievements. Staying humble and grateful will not only keep you grounded but also attract more positive opportunities and collaborations.

5. Keep Learning and Growing

NEVER STOP LEARNING and growing as an online entrepreneur. Use your milestones as a reminder to invest in your personal and professional development. Attend conferences, workshops, and webinars to stay updated with industry trends and acquire new skills. The more you invest in yourself, the more equipped you'll be to tackle future challenges and achieve even greater milestones.

Conclusion

CELEBRATING MILESTONES and achievements is an essential part of the online entrepreneurial journey. By recognizing and commemorating your progress, you can gain a renewed sense of motivation, inspire others, and leverage your achievements for continued success. Whether it's through reflection, sharing your success, treating yourself, hosting a celebration event, or giving back, find ways to celebrate that resonate with you and align with your values. Remember to use these celebrations as a springboard for growth, setting new goals, sharing your journey, staying humble and grateful, and investing in your personal and professional development. Embrace the journey, celebrate your milestones, and continue to thrive as an online entrepreneur.

10.4 Sustaining Long-Term Success

———

S ustaining long-term success is a crucial aspect of online entrepreneurship. It involves consistently adapting to changes in the digital landscape, staying ahead of the competition, and continuously improving your business. In this section, we will explore strategies and practices that will help you sustain your success and ensure the growth and profitability of your online venture.

10.4.1 Embracing Innovation and Adaptation

INNOVATION AND ADAPTATION are key to sustaining long-term success in the online business world. Technology and consumer preferences are constantly evolving, and as an online entrepreneur, it is essential to stay ahead of these changes. Embrace innovation by keeping up with the latest trends, technologies, and industry developments. This will allow you to identify new opportunities, improve your products or services, and stay relevant in the market.

Adaptation is equally important. As your business grows, you may encounter new challenges and face different market conditions. Being flexible and adaptable will enable you to adjust your strategies, products, and services to meet the changing needs of your target audience. Regularly assess your business model, identify areas for improvement, and be willing to make necessary changes to stay competitive.

10.4.2 Cultivating Customer Loyalty

BUILDING A LOYAL CUSTOMER base is essential for sustaining long-term success. Loyal customers not only provide repeat business but also become advocates for your brand, helping you attract new customers through positive word-of-mouth. To cultivate customer loyalty, focus on delivering exceptional customer experiences at every touchpoint.

Provide personalized and responsive customer service, listen to your customers' feedback, and address their concerns promptly. Offer loyalty programs, discounts, or exclusive perks to reward your loyal customers. By building strong relationships with your customers and consistently exceeding their expectations, you can create a loyal customer base that will support your business for years to come.

10.4.3 Investing in Continuous Learning and Development

THE DIGITAL LANDSCAPE is constantly evolving, and as an online entrepreneur, it is crucial to stay updated with industry trends and developments. Investing in continuous learning and personal development will help you stay ahead of the curve and sustain long-term success.

Stay updated with industry news, attend webinars, conferences, and workshops, and join relevant online communities and forums. Engage in networking and collaboration with other entrepreneurs and industry professionals to exchange ideas and gain valuable insights.

Continuously develop your skills and knowledge to adapt to new technologies, marketing strategies, and business practices.

10.4.4 Fostering a Culture of Innovation and Creativity

TO SUSTAIN LONG-TERM success, it is important to foster a culture of innovation and creativity within your organization. Encourage your team members to think outside the box, experiment with new ideas, and contribute to the growth and improvement of your business.

Create an environment that values and rewards innovation. Provide opportunities for your team members to share their ideas and collaborate on projects. Encourage a culture of continuous improvement by regularly reviewing and refining your processes, products, and services. By fostering a culture of innovation and creativity, you can stay ahead of the competition and sustain long-term success.

10.4.5 Monitoring Key Performance Indicators (KPIs)

MONITORING KEY PERFORMANCE indicators (KPIs) is essential for sustaining long-term success. KPIs provide valuable insights into the performance of your business and help you make data-driven decisions. Identify the key metrics that are most relevant to your business and regularly track and analyze them.

Some common KPIs for online businesses include website traffic, conversion rates, customer acquisition costs, customer lifetime value, and return on investment (ROI) for marketing campaigns. By monitoring these KPIs, you can identify areas for improvement, measure the effectiveness of your strategies, and make informed decisions to sustain and grow your business.

10.4.6 Building Strategic Partnerships

BUILDING STRATEGIC partnerships can be instrumental in sustaining long-term success. Collaborating with other businesses or influencers in your industry can help you expand your reach, access new markets, and leverage each other's strengths.

Identify potential partners who share similar target audiences or complementary products or services. Develop mutually beneficial partnerships that allow you to cross-promote each other's offerings, collaborate on marketing campaigns, or share resources and expertise. Strategic partnerships can help you tap into new customer segments, increase brand visibility, and sustain long-term growth.

10.4.7 Staying Agile and Resilient

THE ONLINE BUSINESS landscape is dynamic and unpredictable. To sustain long-term success, it is important to stay agile and resilient in the face of challenges and setbacks. Embrace a mindset of continuous improvement and be willing to adapt your strategies and approaches as needed.

Develop resilience by learning from failures and setbacks. Use them as opportunities for growth and improvement. Stay focused on your long-term vision and goals, but be flexible in your approach. By staying agile and resilient, you can navigate challenges, seize opportunities, and sustain long-term success in the ever-changing online business landscape.

Sustaining long-term success in online entrepreneurship requires a combination of innovation, adaptation, customer loyalty, continuous learning, fostering a culture of creativity, monitoring KPIs, building strategic partnerships, and staying agile and resilient. By implementing these strategies and practices, you can ensure the growth, profitability, and longevity of your online venture.

Also by imed el arbi

Metamorphosis Mindset: Transforming Your Life, One Thought at a Time
Life Mastery: a Toolkit for Success
Your Hidden Power of Mind: Unleashing Your Full Potential
Rise to Radiance
Realize Your Ultimate Potential
Revitalize Your Reality: The Art of Life Transformation
Transforming Within: A Path to Personal Evolution

YouTube Secrets
YouTube Secrets: Build a Successful Channel in 5 Days
YouTube Secrets: Build a Successful Channel with Artificial Intelligence
YouTube Secrets: the Ultimate Guide to Creating Popular and Successful Content

Standalone
The Magical Woodland Adventure

The Money Mindset Makeover: Unleashing True Financial Potential
Digital Deception: A Detective Jane Miller Mystery
The Enigma of Slytherin's Legacy
Bound by Love and Betrayal: an Immigrant's Journey
Tesla's 369 Revelation: A Journey to Spiritual Power
Silencing the Inner Critic: Unleashing Your True Potential
Smoke-Free Success: a Path to Health and Wealth
Navigating Success: 7 Principles of High Achievers
Charm 101: the Art of Wooing Women
Motivate Your Mind: Mastering Motivation for Success
Enchanting Cities: Exploring the World's Urban Treasures
How to Build a Successful Career in the Gig Economy
Mindful Living in the Digital Era
Raising Resilient Kids: a Mindful Guide to Parenting
The Compassionate Self: Cultivating Kindness Within
The Science of Happiness: The Pursuit of Joy
Freelance Writing Success: Launch, Grow, and Scale Your Career
Emotional Well-being: A Guide to Mental Health
HABITS RICH PEOPLE WON'T TELL YOU
Rich Habits, Rich Life: Mastering the Art of Wealth Building
Rising Horizons: Accelerating Business Development
The Lost City of Mythica: Uncovering Mythica's Secret
Generational Harmony: Winning Through Diversity
Alchemy of the Soul: A Roadmap to Life Transformation
Rise Strong: Embracing Resilience and Renewal
AI Riches: Unleashing the Profit Potential of Artificial Intelligence
Building Your Online Store with WooCommerce
Online Entrepreneurship: Success Roadmap

Shopify Mastery: The Ultimate Guide to E-commerce Success

Milton Keynes UK
Ingram Content Group UK Ltd.
UKHW010732241123
433194UK00001B/43

9 798223 700852